ENDORSEMENTS

It's human nature to want everything we pray for right now. What we must understand, however, is that God's timing is not always our timing. The scripture says, "The vision is for an appointed time...and it will surely come." It is telling us that we must wait patiently, and we should be prepared. In essence, don't just wait, but wait well. This principle is the subject of a wonderful book, *Don't Waste the Wait* written by my nephew, Geoffrey Graff. Geoffrey is a brilliant young pastor, a man of exceptional character, and an emerging leader in this generation. I believe Geoffrey's book will motivate and inspire you to move confidently in God's will and to realize His destiny for your life.

Joel Osteen
Pastor, Lakewood Church
Houston, Texas

Geoffrey Graff's book, *Don't Waste the Wait,* is a powerful encouragement not to waste a single minute of experience along the path of life. Many people fantasize about a future event when life will be better, and they miss what God is wanting to do in them, through them, and for them at the present moment. In Geoffrey's book, he helps you understand what steps to take so you don't waste one moment of the "wait" you are perhaps in right now. Remarkably, he also demonstrates that to Jesus, greatness does not mean being the greatest, and this, I think, is one of the most profound messages in this helpful book. I highly recommend it and believe God will use it to encourage and strengthen your life!

Rick Renner
Minister, Author, Broadcaster
Moscow, Russia

Don't Waste the Wait is a timely and hope-filled guide for those navigating seasons of uncertainty or transition. Geoffrey Graff's voice is fresh and faith-filled, helping readers see waiting not as wasted time, but as sacred ground for growth and preparation. This book will encourage your heart, sharpen your focus, and strengthen your trust in God's perfect timing. I recommend this book to anyone needing encouragement in the in-between. Your wait doesn't have to be wasted, it can be the very place God forms you for lasting impact.

Dr. William M. Wilson

President, Oral Roberts University

Geoffrey has written the kind of book every believer needs in their back pocket during life's "in-between" seasons. *Don't Waste the Wait* is overflowing with biblical wisdom, practical insights, and spiritual encouragement for anyone stuck between the promise and the payoff. With conviction, Geoffrey shows us that waiting isn't wasted when we learn to Watch, Act, Improve, and Trust. Whether you feel forgotten in a pasture like David, a prison like Paul, or simply wondering what's next, this book will help you wait on the Lord and walk faithfully all the days of your life.

Keenan Clark

Evangelist

Geoffrey Graff masterfully transforms one of life's most frustrating experiences—waiting—into a sacred opportunity for growth. In *Don't Waste the Wait,* he reveals that our seasons of uncertainty aren't roadblocks but preparation grounds for God's purposes. Through his practical WAIT framework (Watch, Act, Improve, Trust), Graff equips readers with biblical wisdom and actionable steps to navigate transition seasons with peace and purpose. If you're feeling stuck between

God's calling and your current reality, this book will help you discover that waiting isn't wasted time—it's preparation time.

Noah Herrin
Pastor, Way Church
Nashville, Tennessee

Most people equate waiting with wasting time. However, how we wait determines how much the glory of God is displayed in our lives. That's why Jesus commanded the disciples to "wait in Jerusalem" instead of engaging in a lifestyle where they tried to fulfill the Great Commission in their own effort. Congrats to Pastor Geoffrey for helping us experience the great worth of waiting God's way!

Jim Graff
Pastor, Faith Family Church
President, The Significant Church Network

Geoffrey Graff has been living out this message since he was a teenager, recognizing the calling of God on his life but also understanding the importance of waiting and trusting God's timing. I've watched him not waste the wait while he has served his father and others in ministry, and laid dreams on the altar to trust God's timing. He is a mighty man of God and a fresh voice in this hour in the church! I believe in Geoffery and I believe in this message—and I know it will inspire and encourage you in your own journey of waiting and growing into who God called you to be. Don't wait to buy this book, get it today to start making the most of your wait!

Paul Daugherty
Pastor, Victory Church
Tulsa, Oklahoma

I've had the privilege of knowing Geoffrey's family for more than 20 years and have witnessed firsthand his growth and commitment to the calling of God on his life. It's clear that he is becoming one of the standout church leaders of his generation. Through both Scripture and personal experience, Geoffrey has learned the value of waiting on God. *Don't Waste the Wait* is a powerful and timely resource that will equip and inspire you to embrace seasons of waiting with peace, purpose, and faith.

John Nuzzo

Founding Pastor, Victory Family Church

Cranberry Township, Pennsylvania

DON'T WASTE THE WAIT

DON'T WASTE THE WAIT

4 STEPS TO TAKE WHEN GOD'S TIMING FEELS TOO SLOW

GEOFFREY GRAFF

All emphasis within Scripture quotations is the author's own.

Published by Harrison House Publishers
Shippensburg, PA 17257

ISBN 13 TP: 978-1-6675-1164-1
ISBN 13 eBook: 978-1-6675-1165-8
ISBN 13 HC: 978-1-6675-1287-7
ISBN 13 LP: 978-1-6675-1288-4

For Worldwide Distribution, Printed in the U.S.A.
1 2 3 4 5 6 7 8 / 30 29 28 27 26

DEDICATION

To Eden, words could never do justice to the impact you have on my life and ministry. You're my best friend. My safe space. My sounding board for every single chapter of every single section of this book. You are the one I want to wake up to and come home to. We are a team. The best duo to ever exist if you ask me. And I don't want to ever be on another team. Thanks for the love and grace that enables me to become a better man.

To my dad, I hear your voice and guidance in my head every day. I quote you multiple times a week. Thanks for being a great dad. Whatever I do, I know I stand on your shoulders.

To the youth and young adults at Faith Family Church in Victoria, Texas, you weren't a stepping stone—you were a training ground. Thank you for giving me grace and letting me grow while pastoring you. I'll always carry those years in my heart with so much love.

To Overflow Church, I already love you. I can't wait to see what God does through us together. Thank you for letting me be part of your story—the best is ahead.

To you the reader, I'm not some influential person, I just love Jesus and believe the words in this book with all my heart. Thank you for giving it a chance. I've prayed this helps you trust Jesus more—He's got you in the palm of His hand. We're in this together.

CONTENTS

FOREWORD

by Dodi Osteen

This book, *Don't Waste the Wait*, is absolutely wonderful. It is filled with timeless truths and heartfelt encouragement that I believe will help so many people who find themselves in a season of uncertainty, in-between moments, or disappointment. Waiting is never easy. Whether you're waiting on a dream to come to pass, healing to take place, direction to become clear, or simply trying to understand what God is doing behind the scenes—we all go through times when life doesn't unfold the way we thought it would. That's why I'm so thankful this book was written.

We often pray, hope, and plan with the best of intentions, believing that everything will line up the way we imagine. And sometimes, it does. But other times—many times—things don't go the way we expected. Life can surprise us, challenge us, and even bring us to our knees. It's in those moments of waiting, when we're tempted to feel forgotten or discouraged, that we must remember one unshakable truth: God's ways are higher than our ways, and His thoughts are far greater than ours.

Isaiah 55:8-9 (NKJV) reminds us, "'For my thoughts are not your thoughts, neither are your ways my ways,' declares the Lord. 'As the heavens are higher than the earth, so are my ways higher than your ways and my thoughts than your thoughts.'" I've lived long enough to know how true that is. We may not always understand what God is doing in the moment, but we can trust that He is always working—shaping, preparing, and leading us in love. He sees the future when all we can see is the next step. He knows what's best for us even when we're unsure.

This book points us back to that kind of trust. It teaches us to embrace the waiting, not as wasted time, but as a holy season where God is active, refining us, and drawing us closer to Him. The wait is not punishment—it's preparation. It's not a delay in God's plan, but it's often part of His plan. Sometimes the greatest growth, maturity, and transformation happen not in the moment the prayer is answered, but in the time we spend learning to lean on Him before it is.

I believe this book will help you view your wait through the lens of faith. It will lift your head and stir your heart to believe again. It will encourage you to not give up, not give in, and not lose sight of God's goodness even when the path ahead looks uncertain. If you're holding on to a promise, this book will help you hold on tighter—not in your own strength, but in God's strength.

As Geoffrey's grandmother, I couldn't be more honored to introduce this book to readers. I've watched him walk through his own seasons of waiting with grace, courage, and steadfast faith. And now he is turning his story into a source of strength for others. That's what the kingdom of God is all about—taking what we've walked through and using it to bless someone else.

So to anyone who picks up this book: read it with an open heart. Let it minister to your spirit. Let it remind you that God is not done with your story. He's still writing it—even in the waiting.

And remember, God's will is always the best way to live.

Always.

With love,

Dodie Osteen

Geoffrey's proud Grandmother

INTRODUCTION

WE HATE THE WAIT

So, I've come to a conclusion: *We hate to wait.* Let me be clear, when I write of "waiting," I don't mean that blissful down time when we put our head on the couch or toes in the sand and do nothing.

This is what I mean: You go to a restaurant, and if the parking lot is full, you typically go ask the greeter, "How long is the *wait*?" And for me, if I'm told more than 20 minutes, I'm out. I'll get too hangry during that wait.

What about the doctor's office? There are few things that annoy me more than waiting at a doctor's office. Everyone looks sick, they always have the most obscure TV program on, and there's always that one kid with the runny nose who just won't stop looking at me.

But restaurant owners and doctor's offices know we hate the wait. That's why they give us things to do. You remember when you were a kid at a restaurant? It was amazing. While you're waiting for your mac and cheese, you got a little kid coloring menu. Why? To give you something to *do* during the wait. (Can we normalize coloring menus for adults? Just a thought.)

Think about the doctor's office. There are always a plethora of magazines. Truthfully, the only time I read magazines is at the doctor's office. I get all excited about *Better Homes and Gardens,* acting like I "can't wait" to get my lawn in tip-top shape. I'm not excited, I'm just bored. I just hate the wait.

Why do restaurants and doctor's offices give us something to do during the wait? Because they know the wait is more bearable if we have something to do while we're in it. God knows that too. God always gives you something to do while you're in a waiting season. His will is never for you to be bored and unproductive, blaming the inactivity on a season of waiting.

Did David do nothing while he waited to be king? Absolutely not. Did Paul do nothing while he waited to get out of prison? Absolutely not. Did Jesus do nothing while He waited to die on the Cross for the sin and salvation of humankind? You get the point. But we'll dive into these stories in depth later. Right now, my point is simple—you don't have to waste the wait.

You're Probably Waiting

Truthfully, I think you're in a season of waiting. Actually, I think most people are waiting for something. Let me explain. High school kids are walking around thinking, *Man, I can't wait to get outta here! College is going to be sweet!* But until then, they're just waiting. College kids are sitting thinking, *Man, I can't wait to actually get a job and start making some money!* But until then, they're just waiting. And then the college kids get jobs and it's finally perfect, right?

Who are we kidding? That's when the real fun starts and they say, "I can't wait to get a promotion." Or, "I can't wait to get transferred." Or, "I can't wait till my husband gets a promotion so I can stay home with the kids who are a full-time job themselves!" Or, let's be honest, "I can't wait to retire!"

See what I mean? We all have some idea of where we want to be, but we don't just wake up and get there. We wait. And wait. And wait. Waiting seasons are unavoidable, and yet we often don't know how to wait well.

Getting To and Getting Through

We spend so much of life either "getting to" or "getting through." Does any of the following sound familiar: "Ugh…if I could just *get through* high school and *get to* college." Then you get there and what happens? "Ugh, if I could just *get through* school and *get to* a job." And then you're there. "Ugh, if I could just *get through* this position and *get to* another position." And then you're there. "Ugh, if I could just get *through this* week and *get to* the weekend." We all have the temptation of being so fixated on "getting to" or "getting through" that we are missing the opportunity of being *fully in* where God currently has us.

I know you're waiting. And when that time comes for you to move on, that's great. But in the meantime, God always has something for you to do in your waiting season. But we often waste the wait.

The Book in One Chapter

If you are great at starting books and horrible at finishing them (like me), I'll give you the premise of the book in one chapter. You're welcome. I got the idea for this book from a lesser known story about the apostle Paul in Acts 24 where he gets falsely accused of starting riots and arguing with people. So they put him on trial in front of the Roman procurator named Felix. Felix is like a judge for the Roman empire. When Paul presents his case, Felix is indecisive. He ordered that Paul stay in custody so he could have more time to think about what to do with him (Acts 24:22-23).

Every now and then, Felix would go back and check on Paul. Felix would also bring along his wife Drusilla (mother of Godzilla. Just kidding). Felix and Drusilla were curious about the God Paul preached about, but they didn't want to make any serious commitments. They were on the fence about Christianity and on the fence about what to do with Paul. They procrastinated and procrastinated and procrastinated (Acts 24:24–25).

Now, this is where I got thrown off. Acts 24:27 (NLT) says:

> After ***two years*** went by in this way, Felix was succeeded by Porcius Festus. And because Felix wanted to gain favor with the Jewish people, he left Paul in prison.

In the Bible it's one brief verse. In real life it was *two years* that Paul sat in that prison. This wasn't a prison where he could write books, either! Paul was just *waiting.*

That's when God started dealing with me. If anyone had an excuse to procrastinate and waste the wait, it was Paul. What could he really do *waiting* in that prison cell? If anyone was ever in a "waiting season," it was Paul.

Yet God showed me how Felix was a *free man procrastinating* while Paul was a *prisoner being proactive*—still preaching and witnessing for Jesus in that jail cell. When I realized this, God started to deal with me about how I handle those times in my life when I feel like I'm "waiting;" seasons when I know I'm doing something temporary. Seasons when I know I'm not always gonna be doing ______. One day I'm going to ______. But until then, I'm just waiting.

It may be true that we are often waiting, but I learned from Paul that there's a right way to wait. I think we often waste our wait, and then aren't prepared to move on from it when the time comes. So in this book, I show you four things you can do *right now* so you don't waste the wait: ***Watch, Act, Improve, and Trust.*** Take the first letter of each word. What's it spell? WAIT. Just a quick trick to help you remember.

WATCH

The first section is about how we must "watch" in the wait. We examine how to keep our eyes open for the opportunities we have, even if they're not the opportunities we want. I promise, God can use *anything* to teach you, if you keep your eyes open. But so many times we're discontent in the season we're in, throw up our hands in frustration, and in turn close our eyes to opportunities.

Maybe you're thinking, *What opportunities? My job is literally pointless and unrelated to what I actually want to do with my life. Or, I've reached as high as I can go, I'm at a dead end.* Trust me, I've been in both of those positions. Still, there is always some opportunity for us to watch for in our waiting seasons. It may not be the opportunity you want, but our job is to be faithful with the opportunities we have, even if they're not the ones we want. Why? Because God teaches us lessons in those frustrating, waiting seasons.

This is exactly what we see with Paul in prison. He can't go preach to the world like he wants to. His body is locked up, but his eyes are open. Watching for the opportunity he has, even if it's not the opportunity he wants, he sees the opportunity to reach Felix and his wife. Does he want more opportunity? Of course. However, he knows not to throw away the opportunity he has because it's not the one he wants. In others words, Paul knows this truth: ***Good waiting always starts with good watching***.

We must know this, too. We must learn to say, "Lord, I know something else is coming later, but open my eyes to what I need to see now." God can show you lessons in the wait, if you will learn to watch.

After I graduated college with a degree in biblical literature, I worked at Ralph's Grocery Store. Talk about a waiting season. I was supposed to preaching the good news, and yet here I was bagging the canned goods. I was walking around with a highlighter-yellow vest chasing all the carts that people were too lazy to return to the cart area (yeah, I'm still working through my anger. Just return your carts people!).

Yet, God taught me lessons in that season because I watched. For instance, my boss was mean. She would never listen to the employees. When she was wrong, she never apologized. I saw how the team would deflate during their shifts and dread coming to work. Still, I learned valuable lessons during that season. I remember saying to myself, "If I'm ever anyone's boss, I want to be quick to listen and quick to apologize."

I didn't know then that two years later I would actually have a small team I led as the youth pastor in Victoria, Texas. But there was a moment when it hit me: I was a better *leader* at Faith Family Church because I was a *watchful employee* at Ralph's Grocery Store. At the time I didn't see how it was connected, but with God, life's moments are always connected. He wastes *nothing*.

God will teach you lessons in any season if you watch. Some complain that the season we're in is pointless, but really our eyes are closed. One more time: *Good waiting starts with good watching.*

Did you know other parts of the Bible hint at this truth too? For instance, Psalm 130:6 (NASB) says:

> My soul ***waits*** in hope for the Lord more than the ***watchmen*** for the morning; yes, more than the ***watchmen*** for the morning.

This scripture compares waiting on the Lord to being like a watchman. What did watchmen do? You guessed it. They watched! During the night, while everyone else was cozied up in bed, they were alert. They knew morning was coming, but until then they watched to see what needed to be done. They watched for threats. They watched for opportunities to help others. This, my friend, is how you should wait too—just like a watchman.

In this section, I list three specific areas to watch. This list is by no means extensive, but these three areas are ones I have to watch super closely in my own life. They're things you need to be watching too if you want to wait well. In this section we are going to learn to watch for *greatness,* watch for *giants,* and watch for *growth.*

ACT

The second section of the book is about how we must "act" in the wait. Far too often Christians justify a passive lifestyle. We use "churchy" phrases like "waiting on the Lord," wasting our wait and calling it "faith." Waiting and acting seem like opposites, don't they? They're not. I am here to tell you that *the wait is always active.* As you'll read in this section, many people in the Bible needed to act in their current season of waiting to unlock doors for the next season.

Again, it's what we see with Paul in prison. Paul kept his eyes open, *and* he kept his hands active. When most people talk about Paul in prison, they mention how he wrote many incredible letters there. However, Paul didn't write any letters while imprisoned for two years in this particular prison. I think that's why there are not many discussions about this imprisonment.

Still, Paul was active, working on what God called him to do. Paul preached the gospel to Felix and Drusilla time and time again. We don't know the full outcome of Paul's preaching, but we do know the Holy Spirit worked in their hearts. These two nonbelievers became gripped with conviction (Acts 24:25). Paul may not have "sealed the deal" with the salvation prayer, but he put a little pebble of conviction that would probably stick with Felix and Drusilla a long time. Why? Because he was active in the wait. And as you'll see later, God was simultaneously preparing Paul for what came next. That's just God's M.O. (Modus Operandi).

Throughout the Bible, we see God using *active* people. When God called David to be the king, what was David doing? Faithfully taking care of sheep. Why? Because it was the preparation that would help him faithfully take care of a nation. It didn't seem related at the time though, did it?

When God called Peter, James, and John, what were they doing? Fishing. Why? Because it was the preparation they needed before they stepped into being *"fishers of men"* (Matthew 4:19). It didn't seem related at the time though, did it?

When God called Moses, what was he doing? Living in the wilderness, taking care of sheep. Why? Because he was called to help tend to the Israelites in the wilderness. But it didn't seem related at the time, did it? I'll stop, because this is merely the Intro. However, let me say one more brief word; it's not about Paul, the disciples, or Moses. Let me talk about *you*.

God is using your activity now to prepare you for what's next, too. Even when it doesn't seem related, God in His sovereignty has a way of making it work together. The worst thing we could do is do nothing. When we do nothing, it is an indicator of weak faith. We *walk* by faith. Sit? Stand? Lay? Nope—*walk*. Activity is a sign of our faith. Being faithful in the small stuff we can understand is the beginning of seeing God move in the larger aspects of life we can't understand.

I am always amazed at how many people find reasons to become and remain stagnant. In this section I talk about some of those reasons. We'll talk about how we refuse to act because we think we need more *clarity*, because we are stuck in *comparison*, and because we are stuck in *condemnation*. This might be my favorite section. I hope you stick around for it.

IMPROVE

The third section is about how we must "improve" in the wait. God has given you incredible gifts and talents. Here's the problem: God gives gifts like Ikea gives furniture. Have you ever been to Ikea? My wife loves it. I get anxious and want to head straight for the Swedish meatballs. What furniture store has meatballs? That should tell you how large and overwhelming this furniture store is. I remember browsing hundreds of furniture items. After about six lifetimes, Eden selected one. *Finally,* I thought, *we can go home and sit on this chair we just bought.* Except for…we couldn't.

See, Ikea gave us a box and technically all the furniture pieces were in there, but it was our job to assemble them. Again I say: God gives gifts like Ikea gives furniture. Everything you need is inside you, but it's your job to put it together. It's your job to *improve* with the gifts and talents God put within you.

Again, we see Paul *improving* during his imprisonment. Sure, he didn't write a letter in this cell. But what if I told you that this jail cell helped prepare him for what was next. Paul could confidently step into his next season because he was willing to *improve* in his wait.

We can't get the full effect of this story in Acts chapter 24 without reading it in the context of chapter 23. In chapter 24, Paul is sitting in a jail cell where he would be for two years. However, in chapter 23, Paul was having a conversation with God! What was the nature of the conversation?

I'm glad you asked:

> That night the Lord appeared to Paul and said, "Be encouraged, Paul. Just as you have been a witness to me here in Jerusalem, you must preach the Good News in Rome as well" (Acts 23:11 NLT).

God basically tells Paul, "Hey buddy, I'm going to send you across the sea, and you're going to preach all throughout Rome!" Yet, in the *very next chapter,* Paul's in a jail cell in Caesarea. He's more than 1,000 miles away from where God *just* called him. And he would stay in that jail for over two years. He's supposed to be a preacher in Rome, now he's a prisoner in Caesarea. He could have made so many excuses to give up, but Paul chose to improve in the wait. What do I mean?

I mean this: Paul couldn't speak to all of Rome in that prison, but he could speak to Felix, the Roman officer. It's kind of funny; Paul had the opportunity to "practice" in prison, trying out his sermons and logic on Felix, the Roman. In some ways, Felix was a guinea pig that helped Paul improve and prepare for what was next.

Paul couldn't cross the sea and preach to the people in Rome, he was locked up! But he could cross the cell and preach to one Roman. He who is faithful with little will be given much. Paul did get to Rome eventually. And I believe there may have been a point when he was preaching in Rome, and he thought of Felix. At that moment, maybe he thought, *Wow, the prison prepared me for this? Thank God I chose to improve in my wait!*

I believe you'll have your own version of that opportunity and moment. I believe you'll look back at seasons when you chose to improve, even though it seemed useless. I believe you will look back on the sovereign hand of God guiding you the whole time. I believe, looking in retrospect, you will say, "Woah! *That* job prepared me for this? *That* breakup prepared me for this? *That* heartache prepared me for this? *That* home life prepared me for this? I thought it wasted time. It was waiting time. God was allowing me to improve in the wait, while He prepared the way."

God is so much bigger and better than we often give Him credit for. God can use everything to show you how much He loves you and how He has a plan to use you. He can use your biggest regrets, the most useless seasons...you name it, and God can use it! If you're working to improve for Him, you better believe God is working in heaven for you as well.

In the third section, we'll talk about how to improve, and we'll look at what keeps us from improving. We'll talk about *pride,* we'll talk about how we have to improve in the *pasture* before we move on to the throne, and we'll look at God's *procedure* for improving us. The third section is going to be helpful.

TRUST

The final section is about how we must "trust" in the wait. The truth of the matter is this: *Waiting tests your trust.* Sometimes "waiting" and "trusting" feel like the same thing, don't they? Did you know in the Hebrew language the word translated as "wait" is also sometimes translated as "trust"? For example, one of the most famous scriptures on waiting is Isaiah 40:31. The New King James version says, *"But those who* ***wait*** *on the Lord shall renew their strength."* But the New Living Translation says, *"But those who* ***trust*** *in the Lord will find new strength."* You see? Waiting and trusting are so similar. If we are going to wait well, we have to trust!

The truth is, none of us are smart enough to pull it all together and make it all work out, but God is. Was Paul smart enough to know everything God was doing while he waited to get out of prison? No way. But God was working. Was David smart enough to know how God was going to move him from tending sheep to ruling people? No. But God was working. These great people of faith simply did their part (imperfectly) and trusted God to work out the rest. We have to learn to do the same.

So in this final section, we will talk about how we have to trust in *transitional seasons,* because transition is confusing. We'll learn how we have to trust in the *Good Shepherd,* because He's always guiding. And we'll learn how we have to trust in the *night shift,* because when we're scared and can't see the way forward, we can trust God cares for us. As we're faithful in the wait, God is 100 times more faithful to do exceedingly, abundantly above all we could ever ask, think, or imagine (Ephesians 3:20). After all, the main story is about Him, right?

With all that said, I pray this book meets you where you are. You're probably waiting in some capacity. I hope this book helps you wait well. God is writing an incredible story through your life. It will involve waiting. But please, don't waste the wait.

How do you ensure you're not wasting it? Well, first you ***watch*** for opportunities. Then you ***act*** in faith and do something. Then you ***improve,*** working at whatever you do with all of your heart. And when you watch, act, and improve, you are waiting in a way that shows you ***trust***. As you do your part, you can bet your life on the fact that God is doing His part.

Ready?

Put them all together.

In the wait I will:

Watch

Act

Improve

Trust

My Prayer for You

I'm very practical. So my prayer is that the principles in each of these sections are catchy and easy to remember. My prayer is that while you're waiting for what's next, you will "watch, act, improve, and trust." My prayer is that you don't waste the wait, because I promise if you're faithful, you'll see God's faithfulness 100 times over.

I also pray that, if you enjoy this book, you'll tell others about it. This is my first book, and I put everything I had into it. I believe in it. I tried to make it super easy to read but also full of substance that will bless you in your journey. Thank you so much for taking time to read it. Now, before we journey on together, I'd like to pray for you:

> *Dear heavenly Father, I may not know the person reading this book, but I know you made them with incredible gifts, talents, and purpose. You made this reader great. You made this individual to be an incredible source of love and strength to their world. It's hard to be in a season of waiting and transition. It's hard to feel like you're doing something that isn't necessarily the end goal. But please allow this book to do far more in this person's heart because of Your strength and Your Spirit.*
>
> *Would You, Lord, help my heart come across well in this book. Help the reader know I am in their corner and I want them to walk in the fullness of what You have for them. But even more, help this person know that You are in their corner. That's what really matters. Help them know You are the God who wastes nothing. You don't waste the wait, Lord. So help us not waste it either. In Jesus' name, amen.*

Alright, let's do this.

SECTION ONE

WATCH

"Good waiting starts with good watching."

1
WATCH FOR GREATNESS

What's on the other side of your waiting? When your waiting season is over, what do you envision yourself stepping into? Odds are, to you, that next thing is great. Maybe it's moving from your current position to having more of an executive role and a seat at the leadership table. Maybe it's not being the teacher's assistant but the actual teacher. Maybe it's not being a youth pastor but leading the church God put in your heart. (I feel you bro—a person can only take the scent of Axe Body Spray mixed with Little Caesar's Pizza for so long.)

Everyone Wants to Be Great

Everyone wants to be great and to step into greatness. However, if we think only of that *next* season as great, it's easy to see our current season as "less than"—less significant, less important, less relevant. I'm here to tell you: *you'll always waste the wait if you view your current season as a "less than" season.*

There is nothing "less than" about being a teacher's assistant. There is nothing "less than" about your job in the middle or at the bottom of the org chart. There is nothing "less than" about a youth pastor compared to the lead pastor.

I was a youth pastor for five years. I'd write some *good* sermons (if I may say so myself), and then I'd preach them to a couple j-hi kids picking their nose on the front row to keep themselves from falling asleep. Eventually, I'd settle for cutting the sermons short and just playing basketball in the gym. Let's face it, I couldn't be as entertaining as the Fortnite video game they played the night before showing up to service.

If that wasn't bad enough, I'd get online and see other youth pastors preaching conferences in packed-out auditoriums. Sometimes, I would think, *One day, maybe I can get there too.* But until that day, I was just waiting. I didn't always see what I was doing as being that great.

That's when God started to deal with me about how I define *greatness.* And when I saw how Jesus defined *greatness,* I realized I was wasting a season where I was called to be great. Not popular. Not famous. Not at the top of the org chart. But great, nonetheless.

In this chapter, you'll learn how to watch for greatness. When you see the ways God's inviting you to be great *right now,* you'll pour yourself into this season instead of wasting the wait. You're called to be great right now, too. So let's do this together.

How We Define Greatness

Our problem is in the way we define greatness. I went to Wikipedia, where all great scholars go (after Chat GPT, of course). I asked Wikipedia to define greatness. Wikipedia defined greatness like this: "Greatness is a concept or a state of superiority affecting a person or object...."[1] You see that? Culturally we define greatness as "a state of superiority."

That makes sense right? When we think of people who are great we ask, "*Who is at the top?*" So when we think of the *greatest* 3-point shooter of all time, we think of someone such as Steph Curry. When we think of the *greatest* businessperson of all time, we may think of Elon Musk. When we think of the *greatest* evangelist of all time, we think Bob and Larry from *Veggie Tales* (Sorry, Billy Graham. Just kidding). But you get the point. We want to be great, but the way we define greatness in society is by asking, "Who's at the top?"

Some of the reason we feel we're in a waiting season is because we don't feel like we are doing anything *great* yet. And some of the reason we don't feel like we are doing anything great yet is because there are other people farther ahead, closer to the top, and they seem to be making a bigger impact.

In other words, *we waste the wait because we think where we are isn't great.* However, the way *we* define greatness and the way *Jesus* defines greatness is drastically different. And if you can see your season like Jesus sees it, it will ignite a passion in you, not a passiveness in you. Passiveness wastes the wait. Passion doesn't waste the wait.

So let's look for a biblical definition of greatness. It was actually the subject of debate in Mark chapter 9. We'll define it by looking at the four Ms:

1. The *myth* of greatness
2. The *message* of greatness
3. The *motive* of greatness
4. The *miracle* of greatness

The Myth of Greatness

In Mark chapter 9, Jesus' own disciples were arguing about who was the greatest:

> Then they came to Capernaum, and when he [Jesus] was in the house he asked them, "What were you arguing about

> on the way?" But they were silent, for on the way they had argued with one another who was the greatest (Mark 9:33–34 NRSVUE).

Jesus doesn't rebuke the disciples for wanting to be great. We're born to be great. But, like the disciples, we don't just want to be *great*, we want to be *greatest*. Or at least, *greater*. The disciples wanted to know who was great*est*, and Jesus didn't like that.

He doesn't like it when you and I do it either, by the way. Still, we want to be better. We want to be stronger. We want to be thinner. We want to be smarter. We want to be richer. We want to be greater. And we want people to notice.

Let me tell you how sin works. Sin takes something pure and good and subtly twists it. So, in the case of greatness, it's good to want to be great! But sin twists it into not about being great—but about being greater or greatest.

Now, maybe you're thinking like Syndrome, the villain from the *Incredibles* (shout-out to all my '90s kids). Syndrome never felt special, so he wanted to make everyone special. Why? Because finally (cue Syndrome's villainous voice), "If everyone's special, nobody is."[2]

Maybe that's what you're thinking. *How can you even be great if you're not greater? If everyone is great, doesn't that mean nobody is? Doesn't greatness depend on comparison? Like Syndrome said, if everyone's great, nobody is. To be great you have to be above other people!*

There, my friend, lies the myth of greatness. *The* ***myth*** *of greatness says: "I have to go up!"* We have to be bett*er*, smart*er*, thinn*er*, rich*er*. The disciples fell into this trap just like us. But ***to Jesus, greatness ≠ greatest.***

Too many people are losing passion in their current season and wasting the wait. Why? Because they look around and other jobs seem better. Other opportunities seem greater. Since their season isn't the great*est,* they fail to see it still has great*ness.* Because of this, we can waste seasons that had so much potential for greatness.

THE MESSAGE OF GREATNESS

I've told you what greatness *is not.* But what does Jesus say that it *is?* Glad you asked.

Jesus says to the disciples in Mark 9:35 (NRSVUE): "*Whoever wants to be* ***first*** *must be* ***last*** *of all and* ***servant*** *of all.*"

Greatness is found in being…last? Jesus isn't teaching us to be worse than everyone else. He's teaching us to think about other people more and to think of ourselves less. In other words, we need less pride and more humility.

As C.S. Lewis wrote, "Humility isn't thinking less of yourself. It's thinking of yourself less." The disciples wouldn't have been arguing about who was greatest if they were thinking about how they could help each other out. So:

The Myth of Greatness: "I Have to Go Up!"
The Message of Greatness: "Actually, Down."

Humility literally means, "to lower oneself." And you know who lowered Himself all the time? You guessed it. Jesus. Jesus washed feet. Jesus took punishment He didn't deserve. Jesus loved enemies. He literally lowered Himself to help other people all the time.

Now, why do Christians worldwide—with different languages, customs, and cultures—all agree that Jesus is so great? Is it because He came in power and dominated us to show His strength? No! It's because He came in humility as the suffering *servant* who took away the sins of the world when He died on the Cross for us. Jesus came down from heaven, humbled Himself, and served people. He redefined what greatness looks like to we humans.

An Experiment of Greatness

I would be willing to bet that, even though you may have bought into the world's definition of greatness, deep in your heart you actually believe Jesus' message about greatness. You know that the greatest people aren't at the top, but are actually the humble ones serving others. Let's do an experiment together:

Think of one of the *greatest* people in your life. No seriously, picture someone in your mind. The greatest person you know. The one who has impacted you more than anyone else. Don't read the next paragraph until you have that person in your head.

Ready? Okay.

Odds are, you thought of someone who has *served* you more than anyone else in the world. If you're like me, odds are you thought of your mom (shout-out to Tamara Ann Graff the GOAT!).

Now, what made that person great to you? Was it the fact that she (if you chose your mother) was better than everyone else in the world? No, what made her great is that she loved you, served you, fed you, clothed you, tutored you, gave you money when you were short, listened to you when you were confused, held you when you cried. Basically, she loved you so well, and that's why she's the greatest to you!

Here's the kicker, I don't care where you are, you have the opportunity to love and serve people *right now*. Before the promotion. Before the career change. Before you have kids. Before you're married. To Jesus, greatness ≠ greatest. When the world's myth of greatness shouts, "I have to go up!" Picture Jesus smiling at you, washing your feet, and hear Him say, "Actually down."

There are going to be people who, when asked to picture who is the greatest person they know, will picture *you*. Not because you had a ton of Instagram followers. Not because you were the richest or coolest. But because you loved them like no one ever had. You *never* have to wait to be great. But you do have to watch for opportunities to be great if you're not going to waste this season.

Allow me to give one more example of how Jesus' definition of greatness is the greatest to exist. I was watching *The Last Dance,* a documentary on Michael Jordan's career. Most people would say Michael Jordan is the greatest of all time. For most people it's either MJ, LeBron James, or me against all those junior high kids during a Sunday morning youth service. It's very debated.

Anyway, Michael Jordan won six championships. Not only that, he never made it to the championship and lost. However, the first several years of his career he couldn't get to the championship, no matter how hard he worked.

In the documentary, the interviewer asked him (I'm paraphrasing), "What changed for you to go from never getting to the championship to winning it six times in a row?" And Michael Jordan said, "I never got any better those years. But I knew if I was going to be a great leader for my team, I had to make them better." He said, "We won not because I was better, but because I *helped them* get better." Is he not saying what Jesus said to some extent? His greatness was really found once he learned how to serve and help those around him.

Remember, the greatest people make *other people* shine. They care to be helpful more than they care to be noticed. Being great isn't about being the star, it's about being the servant. Have I said it enough ways yet? Great. Now that we've talked about the *myth* of greatness and the *message* of greatness, let's talk about the *motive* of greatness.

The Motive of Greatness

After Jesus tells His disciples the message of greatness, He does something bizarre. He really wants to drive home the point about serving. So:

> Then he took a little child and put it among them; and taking it in his arms, he said to them, "Whoever welcomes one such child in my name welcomes me, and whoever welcomes me welcomes not me but the one who sent me" (Mark 9:36-37 NRSVUE).

In the middle of His message about what it means to be great, Jesus brings a toddler into the center of everyone and hugs the little child. Why? He's about to show the motive of greatness.

Picture this with me. Jesus is teaching, then He points at some little kid and says, "Come here." You know how toddlers are. They waddle. They often have their fingers in their mouth. They usually have goo dripping from their nose. So, I picture this waddling, gooey little mess. And Jesus, mid-lesson, smiles and hugs the child before saying anything. It's a visual message within the verbal message.

What's He saying? True greatness isn't *just* about serving people. It's also about *why* you are serving. Because many times our motives for serving are off. We serve the people from whom we want something in return. But Jesus says, "When you really get what greatness is about, you'll serve *even the children.*"

Why? Because children can't pay you back in any way, shape, or form. They have no power. They can't vote. They have no influence. They can't shout your praises from the rooftop, brag on you to people, or repost you to their Instagrams. In fact, let's be honest, children take you for granted! What child comes home and says, "Jeez, Dad. Thanks for keeping the lights on in this place." "Wow, Mom, the way you cooked dinner and squeezed in a little workout, impeccable." Nope. Not a chance.

Jesus is teaching us something about the movie of greatness. He's saying, when you're willing to serve from a heart that doesn't even need recognition, then you're truly on the path to greatness. So, let's continue the greatness definition.

The Myth of Greatness: I Need to Go Up
The Message of Greatness: Actually Down
The Motive of Greatness: Not to Be Seen

We like to be seen. We like likes. We like comments, shares, and while you're at it go ahead and "smash that subscribe button" (said 90 percent of YouTubers). It's not all bad. In fact, it's important to have people who see your work, validate you, and cheer you on. But an over-desire of being seen and validated is dangerous. If you *need* that, almost every season will feel like a "less than" season.

Jesus knows our hearts and our motives (1 Corinthians 4:5). He'd like us to be honest and ask ourselves, "Am I doing what I am doing for the right reason? Am I doing this for His kingdom or mine?" For example, in my own life I have to ask, "Did I preach that sermon so people thought I was impressive or so I can help others?" The question of *why* you do what you do (your motives) is a question between you and God. If you can answer that question with a clean conscience, watch out! You're on the road to true greatness.

Jesus shows us that when we serve with pure motives, a type of miracle happens. Let's bring this chapter home by talking about the miracle of greatness.

The Miracle of Greatness

After Jesus hugs this waddley, gooey toddler, He ends His teaching by saying:

> Whoever welcomes one such child in my name welcomes me, and whoever welcomes me welcomes not me but the one who sent me (Mark 9:37 NRSVUE).

Did you catch that? Jesus is saying whenever you serve someone with the right heart, it is as if you are welcoming *God Himself* into the equation. Living your life this way gets God's eye on you! You get His reward, a lasting reward that makes the reward of people look so incredibly small! Do you want to get the attention of God and feel His presence? Go love and serve people from a heart that could care less if they ever repay you! Put together the definition now:

The Myth of Greatness: I Need to Go Up
The Message of Greatness: Actually Down
The Motive of Greatness: Not to Be Seen
The Miracle of Greatness: So Christ Is Found

God is looking to find people who want to be great the *right way* and for the *right reason*. Even if people don't see it, I assure you God does. God cheers so loudly over the stuff most people overlook. In fact, can I take a second to appreciate you like I believe God does? Okay, cool. Here I go:

> *Thank you to the moms making sure the kids are dressed, fed, tucked into bed, all the while feeling safe and loved. If no one has told you, you're great. Thank you to the dads sacrificing hobbies and working hard so their kid could play little league this year. If no one has told you, you're great. Thank you to the person unrecognized by their boss but still giving 110 percent behind closed doors. If no one has told you, you're great. Shout-out to the bosses, helping their team shine and creating a culture that everyone benefits from but few thank you for. If no one has told you, you're great.*

Can I tell you why Jesus' definition of greatness is so awesome? Because in the God's kingdom, greatness is accessible to *everyone*. You don't have to be popular, powerful, or anything like that! So many people have fear or anxiety because they feel as if they aren't "enough." But God frees us of that burden.

The truth is, if greatness has a lot to do with motives, I think we are going to be so surprised at heaven's jurisdiction of greatness. You know who I think will have great rewards in heaven? Not necessarily the preachers or the powerful businesspeople. Those will be whoever had the heart to say, "Lord, for You I'll serve. For You I'll love. And if it's not recognized by people, I don't care—because I know my efforts will be rewarded by You."

The miracle of greatness is this: when you let go of needing to be recognized by humans, you get God's attention and reward forever. Don't settle for little rewards by subscribing to such an insignificant definition of greatness. Keep pressing on in private. Keep praying hard in the dark. Keep loving, keep serving, keep giving, even when it feels like they don't see. Because last time I checked, people look at the outward appearance, but God looks at the heart (1 Samuel 16:7).

Please don't waste the wait just because this season doesn't feel like a season when you can be great. I promise, you can be great right now. Keep your eyes open, take up Jesus' definition of greatness, and watch for all the opportunities He is giving you to be great right now.

Summing Up

As I started this chapter, I was pretty transparent about some of my flaws as a youth pastor. Remember? I was comparing myself to bigger and better youth ministries, cutting sermons short to play basketball in the gym, not thinking I was doing anything too great, etc. Well, I almost wasted precious time because of that mindset. I taught the message contained in this chapter in the year 2020. What the kids didn't know is I was trying to learn it myself as I taught it to them. Somehow, by the power of the Holy Spirit, God got this message from my head to my heart.

From 2020-2024 the kids had the same youth pastor, but with a brand-new perspective.

At this stage of my life, I've planted a church, published a book, blah blah blah... You know what's funny? I really miss those days schooling Avery at basketball in the gym (she was a sixth-grade girl who, by her eighth grade year, was better than me). I really miss planning worship sets with a 14-year-old named Nick who was more responsible at 14 than I was at 24. I really miss having a bunch of kids over to the house to brainstorm what crazy stuff we were going to do for camp that summer.

I miss those times, because in those times we weren't trying to be great. We were trying to help others and just love them the best we could. We wanted to see kids from broken families know God loved them even though they were confused. We wanted to show kids from Christian families that Jesus wanted them to have *their own* encounter with Him, not just live off their parents' faith. And man, when the focus was on loving people, God would show up! I may not have ever preached to packed-out auditoriums, but make no mistake, we had *church* in that upstairs room of the gym. Our youth ministry wasn't well-known, but dare I say it, we were stinking *great!* What's even crazier is that there were innumerable lessons I learned in that season that prepared me for the one I am in now.

I tell you all this because the enemy tried to lie to me while I was in that season. And odds are, he's trying to lie to you too. The season you're in is not a "less than" season. There is more opportunity than you know. You are called to be *great* right now, but you have to watch for those opportunities. Greatness ≠ greatest. God will teach you lessons that are preparing you for whatever is next if you keep your eyes open. So what are you waiting for? Don't waste the wait, and don't wait to be great.

Now, come with me to the next chapter and where we examine the second thing we must watch for in our waiting seasons.

2

WATCH FOR GIANTS

Growing up, my dad had a zillion sayings. At the time, they annoyed me. Then I got older and realized they were golden nuggets of truth. One of his favorite sayings was, "Your day starts the night before." Let me give you some context to how he would use this saying.

THE NIGHT BEFORE

Let's say I had basketball practice in the morning. I'd be up watching TV and eating a whole zebra's worth of Little Debbie's Zebra Cakes. (No lie, I once ate 16 in one sitting. I'm not proud to share that.) This is when Dad would come in and restore order to chaos. He'd turn off the TV, tell me to put the Zebra Cakes away, and make me go get ready for bed.

To this, I responded, "Yes, Father. What a wise and caring person you are." Pshaw, yeah right. I'd say, "Uggghhh, Dad, it's fine."

Then, he'd drop that golden nugget, "Nope, your day starts the night before."

Now you see how he would use the saying. And do you also see how my chubby, sixth-grade-self hated it? I didn't connect a late night Monday with a half-hearted Tuesday, but Dad did. I didn't see how the "battle" for me to do well in practice actually started with a much smaller "battle" to be in bed and get good rest the night before. But Dad saw it. He knew, "Your day starts the night before."

The point of me reliving my childhood is simply to say this: there are so many small battles that we don't connect to the "big thing" we are waiting for. God has big, milestone moments for you to walk into. But if you don't watch closely, you'll sacrifice the milestone you could walk into because you didn't see the little battles connected to it.

David's Three Giants Before the Giant

To prove this point, let's look at David's life in 1 Samuel 17. When you hear the biblical name David, you probably think of David and Goliath. Most everyone knows this story. David, an underdog shepherd defeats Goliath, the giant from Gath. It's such a well-known story that it's become a universal saying to describe an underdog battle. Defeating Goliath was a milestone moment for David. It launched him into his military career that led to him being king—the "big thing" God called him to do.

However, I don't want to tell you about the battle with Goliath. I want to discuss the *battles before the battle*. That's right, David faced at least three smaller giants that were all connected to his fight with Goliath. These were important battles! In fact, I've always thought it strange that we talk so much about the battle between David and Goliath but skip over the little-giant battles. After all, in 1 Samuel 17, Goliath gets 8 verses of scripture (verses 41-48), but the little giants get 25 verses (verses 16-40). These battles were important! They were giants that, if David didn't watch for them, would have sabotaged his milestone moment with Goliath.

You have milestone moments to step into too. I promise. However, you also have these same small giants that would love to sabotage you. Can you see them? Let me show you them in David's life.

1. The First Little Giant: Hateful Attitudes

David's brothers were all in the Israelite army, but not David. He stayed home with the family's sheep. Except one day, David's dad asked him to run some food to his brothers at the battlefield. The first Uber Eats. David got the food, set on his way, and was shocked by what he walked into.

On his way to drop the food off, David heard Goliath defying the Israelite's God.

Like most little brothers, David was probably used to fighting bigger people. He asked questions about this giant. He wanted to know why Goliath was allowed to speak of God in such a derogatory way and what reward there would be for killing him. However, Eliab overheard him. Remember Eliab? If you don't, Eliab was David's oldest brother whom people expected to be the king. Eliab had some resentment toward his little brother. He was jealous. First Samuel 17:28-30 (NLT) says:

> But when David's oldest brother, Eliab, heard David talking to the men, he was angry. "What are you doing around here anyway?" he demanded. "What about those few sheep you're supposed to be taking care of? I know about your pride and deceit. You just want to see the battle!" "What have I done now?" David replied. "I was only asking a question!" He walked over to some others and asked them the same thing and received the same answer.

David's first enemy he had to deal with wasn't Goliath. It was his own brother. Eliab wanted David gone and out of there. Eliab developed a hatred in his heart toward David. Before anything, David had to deal with hateful attitudes.

Have you ever stopped to think about what would have happened if David would have engaged with Eliab? We know David turned away and didn't let it take too much of his time and attention, but what if he *did* give it a lot of time and attention? What would have happened? What if David stayed with Eliab, tried to prove himself, and gave all his attention to his brother's dysfunction? Would he have even made it to the battle? Who knows. What we do know is that David was wise enough to recognize battles worth fighting and battles worth leaving in God's hands. And we have to be wise enough to do the same thing.

As a pastor, I counsel people *a lot.* I am always surprised at how many people are stewing over what someone else thinks or says about them. At times I want to interject and say, "What does this have to do with what God is calling you to do right now?" I want to tell them that, until I realize that I have done the exact same thing.

If we aren't careful, we can get so obsessed with the people who have hateful emotions toward us that we lose sight of the main goal God is asking us to accomplish. You only have so much energy—are you giving it to what matters?

I could cite case study after case study of people I have counseled on battles not worth fighting. There is a guy I know who married a good Christian gal, but his family hates her. Their hatred for her makes little sense. She is a good person who has stuck by this guy through *a lot.* He's tried to have sit-down talks with his family, but they have pretty much disowned him. As hard as that is on him, there has to be a point where he recognizes that dwelling on their hateful attitudes is going to do nothing but slow him down from moving forward into what God is calling him to do.

I know another young woman who is making a huge difference at work. She loves her job. However, other people are jealous of her. She could sit in their offices and try to appease them, but is that where her energy is best spent?

Don't get me wrong, people matter. Further, God wants us to make every effort to live at peace with everyone (Hebrews 12:14). But even Jesus had moments when He had to skip town because of the hardness of people's hearts toward Him (Mark 6:4, and Paul advises to avoid useless arguments (2 Timothy 2:23-26).

Here's what I'm saying—the devil would love for you to get so caught up on people's opinion of you that you worry more about pleasing them than pleasing God. So how do you watch for the little giant of hateful attitudes and choose not to engage it? How do you know if it's time to make peace or time to turn away from hateful attitudes? I'm glad you asked.

A Filter for Hateful Attitudes

If you read carefully, you notice a few things in Eliab's words to David. To me, they serve as a kind of filter to recognize hateful attitudes. Let's look at them again in 1 Samuel 17:28 (NLT):

> But when David's oldest brother, Eliab, heard David talking to the men, he was angry. "***What are you doing*** around here anyway?" he demanded. "What about those ***few sheep*** you're supposed to be taking care of? I know about your ***pride and deceit.*** You just want to see the battle!"

With these words, Eliab reveals a lot. Namely, he reveals that he is ignorant of the situation, he belittles David's importance, and he assumes David's intentions. I'm an organization freak, so let me break it down like this:

"*What are you doing* around here anyway?" —> Ignorant of David's situation

"What about those *few sheep*" → Belittles David's importance
"I know about your *pride and deceit*" → Assumes David's intentions

I ask my question again: How do you know if it's time to make peace or time to turn away from hateful attitudes? When I am discerning this for myself, I ask these questions: Are they ignorant of the situation? Are they trying to belittle me? Are they assuming my intentions?

If the person seems to have a hateful attitude like Eliab, I pray for them and keep a soft heart toward them, but I don't give them too much of my attention. Not because I'm trying to be petty, but because I won't allow what God has called me to give my attention to be snuffed out by unnecessary contentions. Like David, sometimes we just have to turn away instead of getting stuck there.

I'm curious, could you be giving way too much time, energy, and thought to issues that really don't matter? I would hate for you to waste the wait and not achieve the milestone moments God's called you to because you're engaged in battles He hasn't called you to.

David waited a long time for this milestone moment, and it was almost hijacked by the little giant of hateful attitudes. But he knew how to watch for it, and we have to learn how to watch for it too.

David defeated the first little giant, and now it was on to the next one: King Saul. King Saul didn't necessarily have a hateful attitude toward David, but he did have some pretty bad advice.

2. The Second Little Giant: Unhelpful Advice

David wanted to fight Goliath, and at first King Saul was resistant. To be fair, he had a responsibility as the king. He had to make sure he was sending his best warrior, considering Israel's freedom was on the line. Still, King Saul's words to David reveal something you and I have to watch out for when it comes to the leadership we sit under and advice we listen to.

> Saul replied, "You are not able to go out against this Philistine and fight him; you are only a young man, and he has been a warrior from his youth" (1 Samuel 17:33 NIV).

King Saul told David only what his *weaknesses* were. He only told him who he *wasn't*. Here's the scary thing, many leaders think it is their job to assess people and tell them where they're weak. That may be part of it, but what about people's strengths? The people who have made the biggest difference in my life haven't harped on my weaknesses as much as they have celebrated my strengths.

The problem with leaders or friends who only point out your weaknesses is that eventually, they almost always try to make you just like them. In other words, since they can only see your weaknesses, they feel obligated to impart some of their strengths to you. It's not that they won't let you fight. It's that they try to make you fight just like they would. That's what Saul did.

> Then Saul dressed David in ***his own tunic.*** He put a coat of armor on him and a bronze helmet on his head. David fastened on his sword over the tunic and tried walking around, because he was not used to them. "I cannot go in these," he said to Saul, "because I am not used to them." So he took them off (1 Samuel 17:38-39 NIV).

Saul could only see David's weaknesses. So what did he do? He tried to send him out to battle as a carbon copy of himself. Saul was great with a sword. David was great with a sling. Give Saul a shield. Give David a stone. Two great warriors. Two totally different skill sets.

Can you imagine if David would have tried to fight his battle with King Saul's armor? He would have been destroyed and Israel would have been enslaved. Unknowingly, King Saul was giving him terrible advice! If David would have taken the advice, he wouldn't have succeeded in his milestone moment with Goliath. But David knew how to watch for bad advice.

Leaders, friends, and mentors are very capable of giving bad advice. Do you know how to watch for it?

Bad Advice in Great Availability

It's so much easier for people to tell you your weaknesses rather than your strengths. It's just easier to recognize the bad than appreciate the good, isn't it? Anyone can see a lump of coal, few can find the diamond in it. You need people around you who see the God-given gifts in you and encourage you to be the best version of *you*.

One of the people who has impacted me more than almost anyone in the world is my former youth pastor, Josh Joines. Pastor Josh (or "PJ") is an incredible leader. He pastors a large, life-giving church in Baytown, Texas, that seems to double every few years. He has an incredible leadership gifting. Even when I was a kid in his youth group, he was mobilizing us and empowering us to build a contagious culture. Our youth group thrived under him, and it was so fun to be part of it!

In 2019, about seven years after he had started his own church, I took over the same youth group. It wasn't thriving. Honestly, it was pretty dead, and I was eager to inject some life back into it. Of course, I called PJ to ask his advice. He gave me some great advice, but the best advice he gave me wasn't on that call, it was on a call a few days later.

PJ called me and said something to the extent of, "Hey G, I was thinking about our conversation the other day. I did some good things as the youth pastor, but today is so different. The main thing you have to know is just be yourself and play to your strengths. You have a lot in you, and God didn't make you just like me. The worst thing you could do is to be David trying to wear Saul's armor."

That call gave me *permission*. It gave me a sense of responsibility to not be a carbon copy of what PJ had been, but to pray like crazy, figure out how God made me, and ask God to show me how He needed me to lead the group.

PJ's call also helped me realize another way that made him a great leader. PJ knew how to speak to my strengths rather than just harp on weaknesses. I'm pretty picky about who mentors me. If they criticize more than celebrate, I'm usually out of there. But if they celebrate my strengths more than criticize my weaknesses, you better believe I listen with pen and pad when they have critiques.

Don't Play the Blame Game

Before we move on, let me say this: the last thing I want to do is stir up some kind of bitterness in your heart toward leadership, mentors, or friends. Most people, even the people who zone in on your weaknesses, genuinely want to make you better. They genuinely care about you but don't always know how to care the right way. And truthfully, if you walked through what they walked through, you would probably be sympathetic and understand where they were coming from.

So again, I don't want to stir up bitterness in your heart toward people. Because here is the kicker—it's *your* responsibility to watch for unhelpful advice. It's not everyone else's responsibility to give you perfect advice. Don't blame people for bad advice; take accountability for your ability to sort through it.

I'm a huge fan of the *Rocky* movies. I could quote almost every scene of the series (it's honestly a bit strange). In any case, Rocky starts as an underdog boxer from Philadelphia who shocks the world and eventually wins the heavyweight championship of the world. Throughout the series of movies, he becomes rich, famous, and known as one of the greatest boxers of all time.

However, there is one scene that makes the waterworks well up in my eyes every time. Rocky's son, Robert, grows up living beneath his potential, and he blames his dad. He basically tells Rocky that it's hard to live in his shadow. Everyone expects Robert to be like Rocky. In other words, Robert is blaming Rocky for where he is in life. And then Rocky delivers one of the best monologues in cinema history:

> *Robert, you grew up good and wonderful. It was great just watching you. Every day was like a privilege. And the time came for you to be your own man and take on the world and you did. But somewhere along the line you changed. You stopped being you. You let people stick a finger in your face and tell you you're no good. And when things got hard, you started looking for someone to blame. Like a big shadow.*
>
> *Let me tell you something you already know. The world ain't all sunshine and rainbows. It's a very mean and nasty place and I don't care how tough you are it will beat you to your knees and keep you there permanently if you let it. You, me, or nobody is gonna hit as hard as life.*
>
> *But it ain't about how hard you hit. It's about how hard you can get hit and keep moving forward. How much you can take and keep moving forward. That's how winning is done!*
>
> *Now if you know what you're worth then go out and get what you're worth. But you gotta be willing to take the hits, and not pointing fingers saying you ain't where you wanna be because of him, or her, or anybody! Cowards do that and that ain't you! You're better than that!*[1]

Am I embarrassed that I just used such a long quote from Rocky? Nope. Am I embarrassed I knew it from memory? Nope. Because it's true.

We can all let people stick their finger in our face and tell us what we aren't. And worse, we can blame them for us being stuck in a rut. But guess what? God's not going to judge you one day based on what everyone said about you, He's going to judge you based on what you did with what He gave you.

Do you know what He gave you? Do you know the gifts and talents He put inside you? I promise you, you have some incredible gifts. And it's *your* responsibility to make sure you use them; it's not other people's responsibility to lead you and treat you perfectly.

People aren't perfect, and people aren't thinking about your life and your strengths nearly as much as you're thinking about them (and before you get angry, you aren't thinking about their life and strengths that much either!). Was Saul *bad* for giving David his armor? No! Was it unwise? Yes! So there you have it—people can give unwise advice and not be bad people. It's your job to filter that out. How?

A Filter for Unhelpful Advice

Saul told David two things: *Who he wasn't and what he couldn't do.* To me, that's a good filter for recognizing unhelpful advice. We have to watch for that little giant of unhelpful advice; the type of advice that focuses on who we *aren't* and what we *can't* do.

At the end of the day, if David would have followed Saul's bad advice, he would not have stepped into his milestone moment of defeating Goliath. And if you don't know how to watch for that little giant of unhelpful advice, you won't step into your milestone moments either. Now let's tie up this chapter with that last little giant David had to fight.

People don't always realize that David actually had quite an advantage against Goliath if he played to his strength. Let's do a quick history lesson. In an ancient army there were three main groups: the calvary, the infantry, and the artillery. The cavalry were soldiers who fought on horseback. The infantry were soldiers who fought on foot. The artillery were soldiers who fought long range with slingshots.

Sure, Goliath was a giant. Toe-to-toe, he would have whooped David. However, David was more of an artillery guy. He had a slingshot and fought long range, from the air. Why would he go toe-to-toe? There have been many historians who, when considering this fact, believe David had an advantage. Malcom Gladwell wrote a whole book about it![2]

It's always amazed me how we view David as some helpless little shepherd boy with insufficient ability to do what God called him to do. He didn't view himself like that. If he had, he probably would have never fought the battle and stepped into his milestone moment. And if you view yourself as having insufficient ability to do what God called you to do, you're not going to step into milestone moments either. This is the third little giant David fought, and a giant we must watch for too.

3. The Third Little Giant: Insufficient Ability

Yours and David's Greatest Strength

I don't want to puff up your head here. I'm not saying you can do whatever you want! To my fellow 5' 7" homeboys, you probably aren't going to dunk and you have very slim chances of making the NBA. (If you do, please feel free to throw it in my face with an "I told you so.") What I'm saying is that you are fully capable of doing whatever

God calls you to do. However, it's *not* because you are good enough. It's because, like David, you fight from the air and with a power higher than your own.

Whether David was or wasn't the underdog, it really doesn't matter because he put his trust in Someone beyond his ability. He looked at Goliath and said that Goliath came at him with "sword and spear." So logically, we would expect him to say, "But I come with a sling and stone!" That's not what he says though. Instead, he says he came *"in the name of the Lord"* (1 Samuel 17:45-47). David knew his "X-factor" wasn't a skill he possessed but the name he carried. I wonder if you really believe in the power of the name you carry?

The Power of a Name

Do you realize the power of a name? Growing up, my dad pastored a large church. Our last name is Graff. There were many times I would be in kids' church and I wanted to leave. Or I would be in Vacation Bible School and wanted to skip arts and crafts to go to my dad's office to grab a snack. The workers initially would stop me and say, "Where are you going?" And I would abuse my privilege (I'm not proud of it). I'd say, "I need to go see my dad. It's important." They'd look at my name tag, see the last name, and escort me. Now I'm not saying I was right. I probably wasn't. I'm just illustrating the power of a name. When you "come in the name" of something, there are either advantages or disadvantages of that name. It depends on the strength and reputation of that name.

Now, back to David. Do you see why he came in the name of his God? David knew what others in the Bible knew—in his own strength he had insufficient ability. But in God's strength, he was more than able.

Many people in the Bible walked into milestone moments, *despite their inability*, because they carried God's name. Remember Moses?

God called him to lead the Israelites out of slavery. Moses had many reasons to think he was unable to do this; he made mistakes, he was a murderer, he couldn't speak clearly. Moses tried to get out of his assignment. However, God gave Moses *His name* and the excuses had to go.

In Exodus 3:13–15 God tells Moses his name is *"I Am."* If you're like me, you read that and think, *I am? That's not a name!* But God was stating that He could be whatever we need in our specific situation. He has preeminence and power over all things. So let's get away from Moses and David and get to *you*.

From David to Moses to You

Why do you disqualify yourself and see yourself as unable? You've messed up too much? God would say, "*I AM* your Forgiveness" (1 John 1:9). You don't have the resources? God would say, "*I AM* your Provider" (Philippines 4:19). You don't have the strength? God would say, "I AM your Strength" (Psalm 18:2). You don't have the wisdom? God would say, "*I AM* Wisdom" (Proverbs 2:6).

My point is this: if you don't watch for the giant of insufficient ability, you'll stay stuck in waiting seasons making excuse after excuse about why you can't take another step forward into your purpose. And the truth is, by yourself, you aren't able to step into your purpose! Neither was David and neither was Moses. But they both went forward in the name—the name that knew no limits of love, grace, power, forgiveness, wisdom, reconciliation, and strength.

If you're a believer, you bear *that* name—the name of Jesus. That's a whole lot better than bearing the name "Graff" and getting out of kids' church. His name will get you out of your past and into your purpose. With *His* name, you are more than able. At the end of the day, the story is about His name, not ours. So embrace that family name, realize you have an incredible purpose, and watch for those little giants that try to sabotage it!

Summing Up

I hope you take these little giants seriously. The little giants of hateful attitudes, unhelpful advice, and insufficient ability are sneaky, but they're powerful. I see them defeating people all the time. Far too many people have waited in seasons for too long because they are losing these battles. You're not going to be one of them.

Alright, we've talked about watching for *greatness,* we've talked about watching for *giants,* now let's talk about how to watch for *growth.* This next chapter is painfully good.

3

WATCH FOR GROWTH

I don't know if you're the baby of your family, but if you are, you'll feel very seen reading this paragraph. You see, I am the youngest of four kids. I could rant about how I was picked on, how I couldn't keep up in family sporting events, and how I was given the most lame role in any game we played (shout-out to "plumpy," the Candy Land character I was forced to be). However, today I choose a different rant: hand-me-down clothes. Oh yeah, we're going there.

Big Clothes and Babies

My parents were frugal, so why buy me new clothes when my brother, who is seven years older, has perfectly good clothes sitting in the attic? I get the logic, but here's the truth—the clothes were *barely* cool when Mike wore them, so seven years later they were absolutely horrible! That's not the worst part, though. I'm shorter than my brother, and I didn't grow as fast either. You know what that means? Every time I got "new" clothes, they were too big. They swallowed me. And my parents would say four words I hated, "You'll grow into it."

Now that my wife and I are expecting our first child, I've been getting all the parenting advice I can. One common theme has come up. Wise parents have been telling Eden and I to buy clothes a little bigger than the baby's size. Why? Because the baby is going to grow! If we buy clothes that fit, the baby will quickly grow out of them.

Instead, we should buy clothes a little bit too big. Because after all (as my parents said), they'll grow into it.

A Good Father

What if I told you that God approaches our lives with this mindset? Not with clothes, but with circumstances. God knows your potential. He is the One who created you with all the strengths, weaknesses, and quirks you have. He knows exactly what you're created to do and exactly what you need to grow.

I'm going to ask you a question, and please do not throw the book away after I ask it, deal? What if all the "hard seasons" are God's way of putting you in circumstances that are too big for you, because at the end of the day, your Father knows—you'll grow into it.

As we finish this section on "watching" in the wait, I want to tell you a simple truth. You should be watching for the opportunities that make you uncomfortable. You should watch for the opportunities that scare you. You should keep your eyes peeled for the opportunities that seem a bit big for you. Why? Because all your wildest dreams will come true and you'll succeed at everything your hand touches? Maybe, but probably not. You need to watch for these opportunities because, succeed or fail, you *will* grow.

To be clear, by "grow," I partly mean that you'll grow in your skill set, but I especially mean that you'll grow in your *character*—how much you're like Christ. God cares about the success of your endeavors, but He cares more about the character of your heart. The truth is, only with good *character* can you sustain the dreams God has for you. So growing your skill is important, but growing your character is primary.

Maybe you're called to lead a ton of people, but without *character* you may get insecure when the rest of your team starts doing well and needs you less and less. You may be called to be an incredible teacher, but without *character* you may lose your temper and scar someone you were supposed to impact positively. Do you see what I mean? God wants to put you in situations that grow your skills and character. *God is in the business of blessing the work of your hands, but not at the expense of shaping the character of your heart.*

In this chapter, I share a scripture that explains how God helps you grow into what He's calling you to do and be. This is one of those passages that helped me make sense of many of my own hard seasons. It helped me look back and say, "Ah, now I see why I was supposed to go through that! I did grow into it!" Not only that, but it's also a scripture that helped me watch for the difficult opportunities and take leaps of faith.

You're called to get out of the season you're in eventually, but the road ahead is probably harder than you think. And it's hard because God is the good Father who knows you'll grow into it. Let's talk about James 1:2-5.

JAMES' WORLD

When James wrote this letter, things were really tough on those who believed in Jesus. James probably wrote this in the mid to late 40s CE. He writes it to the twelve tribes of Israel scattered abroad. Do you know why they were scattered? Because persecution had amplified and scattered the people. That's why one of the major themes of James' book is how we handle tough seasons that feel too big for us. Even if our situation isn't tough because of persecution specifically, these words apply to our tough seasons in general.

He says in James 1:2-5 (NLT):

> Dear brothers and sisters, when troubles of any kind come your way, consider it an opportunity for great joy. For you

> know that when your faith is tested, your endurance has a chance to ***grow***. So let it ***grow***, for when your endurance is fully developed, you will be perfect and complete, needing nothing. If you need wisdom, ask our generous God, and he will give it to you. He will not rebuke you for asking.

Did you notice a word that was repeated? That's right, *"grow."* James is teaching us how difficult seasons are the ones that grow us. Here's how.

How *Strength* Is Made

When James says these difficult things cultivate endurance (verses 2-3), he's saying a mouthful. The Greek word *endurance* comes from two words: "remain" and "under."[1] It paints a picture of someone who is under a heavy load. Instead of running from it, they choose to *remain under* it.

Let's have some fun with this.

When It Hurts Remember...

Do you ever go to the gym and squat? I hate it, but I do it every week. Whenever you squat, you load up the bar with a weight that's heavy for you, then what do you do? You put it on your back, step away from the squat rack, and *remain under* that weight. Then, when it gets too light, what do you do next? Add weight. Why? Because we know this is the only way to grow our muscles. This is what James is saying, but he's talking about much more than muscles. He is talking about your character and your calling. Instead of running from those hard things, James in essence telling you—*when it hurts remember:* ***strength is made under heavy weight.***

The Weight in the Wait

Some of us are trying to escape from the *weight* God is trying to give us in the *wait*. You're under something heavy. I get it. There are times you want God to get you out from under it. Maybe He will. But maybe He's allowing you to remain under heavy wait so you grow. Remember: *God's will is not always to help you get out, but it is always to help you grow up.*

The weight of waiting is helping you grow! In fact, James says when we stay under these weights, we are becoming *"perfect and complete"* (James 1:4). That word *perfect* doesn't mean without sin or flaw. It means "mature" and has the connotation of something reaching its end goal. For instance, the "end goal" of an acorn is an oak tree. An oak tree is a "perfect" acorn. You see?

James is saying there is a perfected "end goal" version of you—the version God saw when He formed you. Picture it! There's a version of you who has joy regardless of what happens. A version of you who isn't controlled by emotions. A version of you who isn't so worried about what others think. A version of you who forgives and is free of bitterness. A version of you who is confident and thriving in your gifts. There's an "end goal" version of you!

But guess how you get there? You remain under heavy weight. Now do you see why God is asking you to remain in difficult opportunities? He sees what you can grow into. When you're under those weights, think of God as your Spotter saying, "You got this. I won't let it crush you. You'll grow into it."

What *Wisdom* Knows

What if you can't lift that weight, though? I get it. I've felt like that. Shouldn't we call out to the spotter and say, "Hey! Get this weight off me!" You'd think, if the weight is too heavy, James would tell us to ask for *deliverance*, right? But instead, he tells us to ask God for *wisdom* (James 1:5).

If you're like me, you're thinking, *I don't want wisdom! I want deliverance! Get this stupid weight off me!* So why do we ask for wisdom instead of deliverance? Because if we have *wisdom* to see what God is up to in the hard seasons, we will know He isn't wasting one ounce of our pain. In other words:

When it hurts remember:

1. *Strength* is made under heavy weight
2. *Wisdom* knows this season's not a waste

The God of Leftovers

The older I get, the more I see God doesn't waste anything. Remember when He fed the 5,000? He made the disciples pick up the 12 leftover baskets. Remember when He did it a second time? He made the disciples pick up the 7 leftover baskets. But I'm not here to tell you God doesn't waste food, I'm telling you God doesn't waste *anything* you go through.

I had a friend who was like most college kids…broke! Every weekend, he and his fraternity brothers would take all the leftovers they had from the week. It didn't matter if it was something delicious like steak or disgusting like broccoli (if you like broccoli, that's weird). They would combine it, mix it together, and somehow concoct this "leftover casserole." The strangest part is they loved it! They looked forward to it every week!

God does something similar. When I say He doesn't waste anything, I mean *anything*. I've seen God use seemingly pointless seasons and make something good out of each one. I've seen God use seasons when people tried to hurt me, and He made something good out of it. Want to get real? I have seen God use some of my biggest sins and deepest regrets to form a deeper love for Him in my heart. God is the God who wastes *nothing*. He's not going to waste the hard things He's calling you to or the heavy things He's having you stand under. But we need wisdom to see these times as growth opportunities.

Do you know how much is wasted because people don't have wisdom to see their situation as God sees it? What if God was trying to cultivate patience in you, but you could only see how annoying they were? What if God was trying to teach you forgiveness, but you could only see how wrong they were? What if God was trying to teach you contentment, but you could only see what you didn't have yet? What if God was trying to teach you discipline, but you could only see how nagging your boss was? I'm not saying that the season wasn't hard. I'm saying wisdom reminds us that the season isn't wasted by God. Is it wasted by you? Are you running from opportunities that can grow you?

We shouldn't just want deliverance in these seasons, we should want wisdom. God wastes nothing. He uses these seasons to form the "end goal" version of you He's seen all along. Do you have the wisdom to see that? If so, you won't waste the wait by wasting the weight.

Moldy Medicine

Let me end the chapter by telling you about a scientist named Alexander Fleming. He's the guy you're thankful for but probably don't know about. I'm sure at some point in your life, you've been sick. Not only that, but I am also sure at some point you relied on a drug called penicillin. It's somewhat of a miracle drug that has saved over 200 million lives. Here's the fun part—do you know how it was discovered?

In 1928, physician and microbiologist Alexander Fleming returned to his lab after a vacation. When he walked into the lab, he noticed mold growing in an uncovered petri dish containing a staphylococcus culture. If you're like me, this grosses you out.

Instead of being grossed out, Fleming studied the mold in the dish. He noticed the mold was having an interesting effect on the other bacteria. Eventually, he learned this mold had a substance that produced a "self-defense chemical" and was able to stop harmful bacteria.[2] He named that substance penicillin. Now, penicillin is a medicine used every day to help stop harmful bacteria in the human body. Who would have thought, where most other people saw mold, Fleming saw medicine.

This is the way God works too. God sees so much more in your situation than you can. I'm not denying it: there is definitely a weight in your wait. Some of it is moldy and gross. Yet, in the hard seasons, if we remain under the weight and ask for wisdom, we'll see God wastes nothing. He's bringing beauty from ashes, strength from weakness, medicine from mold. You get the point. We have to watch for growth opportunities in the wait, not run from them! Why? Because God uses them to help you grow.

Putting My Money Where My Mouth Is

Before I end this chapter, I want to say this: I know I'm advocating for you to do something extremely uncomfortable. However, I'm not giving you advice I wouldn't take.

I was in a very cushy situation. My wife graduated Physician Assistant school, started her own medical practice by the beach, and was making *a lot* of money. I was the youth and young adult pastor and quadrupled the programs I was over, then moved into leading all the ministries at the church. I loved the people there, and they loved me. If I would have been the next lead pastor, I don't think there would have been too many objections (though, I'm sure there would have been some). I was on track to be my own boss at a mega church in my early 30s.

Please know, I am not bragging. I am nothing but a culmination of God's grace and wonderful people who have helped me. My point is this: God asked us to leave all that. He asked us to start a church with zero dollars, zero congregants, and move to a city where we knew two people. Why? I believe, for me, leaving was the route that would grow my reliance on God and my character. God cared more about character than comfort.

Getting the church off the ground has been a *heavy weight*. I stepped into a space where I am the chief pastor, chief marketing director, chief fundraiser, chief event planner, chief accountant, chief everything! I couldn't have completely anticipated the weight I'm having to remain under. But my goodness, it has been wonderful. God has taught me so much. He put me in a situation bigger than I could handle in my own strength. But guess what? I'm growing into it.

God has stuff for you to grow into too. Just keep those eyes open. When you sense Him leading you toward something that seems a bit difficult, be willing to jump into it! Why? Because our good Father always puts us in something a little bit too big. Don't worry—you'll grow into it.

The next section of this book is about *acting*. If you're like me, you have questions you need answered before you act: "But what if I'm not 100 percent sure?" "What if other people are better at this stuff than me?" "What if I've made more mistakes than other people I see God using?" I'll deal with all that in the next section of this book. It's probably my favorite section. Ready to act?

SECTION TWO
ACT

"The wait is always active."

4
ACT WITHOUT CLARITY

One of the biggest reasons we waste the wait and remain passive is that we think we need *more* clarity. I'm here to tell you, I think you need *less* clarity. I'll take the long-winded approach of proving this point by telling you about my brother.

My big brother is one of my favorite people in the world, but we are so different. Don't get me wrong, we have very similar senses of humor, hobbies, and interests. Aside from me being way better looking, we are very alike. But at my core, I am a *planner*. I don't say that as a "brag." It's truly just how I'm made. My mom said when I was very young, I would wake up and ask, "Okay mom, what's the plan today?" As early as first grade, the night before school, I would lay all my clothes out perfectly on the floor as if some little person got raptured and left behind his school uniform. I still do it! I pre-make my coffee, pack a lunch, and get my gym clothes and my work clothes all laid out the night before. Why? It takes the guesswork out of my morning! I have insane clarity! What will I eat? Already figured out. What will I wear? Already figured out. Will it be a coffee morning? Yes, always. My brother, Mike, is very disciplined, but he is more of a free spirit.

A European Adventure

When I graduated college, we wanted to take a trip to Europe. It was a way to celebrate before I moved to Los Angeles to pursue my master's degree. Mike came to me with a brilliant plan: We fly into Dublin, Ireland, ten days later we fly home out of Barcelona, Spain—and we would bring only our backpacks. I was pumped! However, I obviously had questions. If you don't know, Dublin and Barcelona are *not* close.

"Mike, how will we get from Dublin to Barcelona in 10 days? How many stops are we making along the way? What cities will we visit on the way? What about hotels?" Surely Mike had phenomenal, thought-out answers, right?

Mike's answer: "Bro, chill. We'll figure it out along the way."

If I didn't trust my big bro so much, there's no way I would have done it. But we did it and sure enough, we made it back in one piece all while having an absolute blast. Was it seamless? No. Was it a little hectic? Sure. I mean, one night we didn't know where to go and accidentally ended up staying with a drug dealer. (Hope you're doing well and not selling drugs anymore, Andy!) Another night, we ended up sleeping on some small train with some Romanian family. We also got stopped, dragged off the night bus, and interrogated by German customs for no real reason. At the end of the day, though, it was one of the most fun trips I have ever taken. My brother would be the absolute worst and best travel agent at the same time.

Your Map and God's Formula

Why do I tell you this story? Because when I initially saw the map and realized how far Dublin was from Barcelona, I freaked out. "How are we going to get from there to there?" I almost didn't even want to go! However, as I took one little step at a time, it all worked out.

A lot of us view our life a little bit like a map. We say, "I'm currently here, but I believe God is calling me there." I don't know where "there" is for you. Maybe it's to attend a particular college, to start a business, to be a mom, to start a side hustle, to be rich and famous.... The possibilities are endless. But when we look at where we *are* compared to where we *feel called to be*, it gets so overwhelming! We go back and forth debating which steps will get us to our destination. And here's the scary part—because we don't know *all* the steps, we often don't take *any* steps.

There are many good Christians who genuinely want to do God's will. Their hearts are so willing. They don't know all the steps, and they think they're waiting on God to reveal them. It's like they're sitting in a parking lot, hands on the wheel, saying, "God, show me and I'll go!" "You want me to empty my bank account and start this business? Just show and I'll go!" "You want me to move to this city? Just show and I'll go!" I used to say this. I had such a good heart. And such bad theology.

We like the "show and I'll go" formula. But I've realized that's not God's formula! You remember Abraham, right? God called him to leave everything and promised to make him the father of many nations. Sounds amazing, but look at the order of God's formula in Genesis 12:1 (NIV): *"The Lord had said to Abram, '**Go** from your country, your people and your father's household to the land **I will show** you.'"*

Did you catch it? I bolded it so you'd see. We say, "God, show and I'll go." Yet, God says, "Go and I'll show." Ouch. We don't like that as much. I wonder why?

The Idol of Clarity

To put it bluntly, I think we have made clarity an idol. I know I have. I remember being paralyzed by a decision. I was praying about it for so long, and God finally showed me my prayers were prayed from a heart of fear, not a heart of faith. I wanted to pray until I knew with 100 percent certainty: *this is God's will!* Let me just be honest, God doesn't usually give 100 percent certainty in anything. And when people say, "You better be 100 percent sure," that's normally bad advice that enables you to waste the wait.

The only thing *biblically* God gives you 100 percent certainty is His faithfulness to take care of you and make you more like Him. So if you succeed or fail, He'll take care of you and make you more like Him. If you pick this city or that city, He'll take care of you and make you more like Him. If you pick this major or that major, He'll take care of you and make you more like Him.

Now if that doesn't make you excited, maybe it's time to look into your heart and ask: An I more excited to have the certainty of success *or* to be shaped into the character of Jesus through whatever comes my way? If you were more excited about the first option, maybe *that's* your real problem. Maybe what you're praying about is competing to be your god over *the* God. When we say, "I don't want to step out until I'm 100 percent sure," my question is, "Why? Because when you're 100 percent sure you won't need God anymore?" What kind of God wants that for you?

We waste the wait so often, desiring clarity when in reality, an over-desire for clarity often reveals an under-developed trust in God.

Yet we make our obsessive need for clarity seem like it's "holy" by calling it "waiting on the Lord" or "waiting in faith." Last I checked, we aren't called to *wait in faith*, we're called to *walk by faith. Walk* is an *active* word. I'm not God, but I think He'd give you the same advice about your journey as He gave Abraham about his (and the same advice my brother gave to me): "Just go! We'll figure it out along the way."

The Rest of the Chapter

I'm not saying you should jump into any and every inclination you have. Of course there is prayer, fasting, waiting, and wisdom involved! You should know *enough* to get moving in a direction with confidence. I think we overemphasize those things so much that we undermine the sovereignty of God.

As believers, I truly think we need to get back to more of a middle position; a position that has less to do with your ability to make every perfect move, and more to do with the sovereign hand of God to guide, guard, protect, and direct those who genuinely want His will. After all, the story of the Bible is about *His* goodness, not ours, right?

So, yes, there is a place to wait. But as I previously said, I believe the wait is active. Another way to say it is like this: *I believe action comes before answers.* I could prove this in the Bible 100 times. So for the rest of the chapter, we look at a story in Acts, and I will show you three actions you can do right now as you wait. Then, I'm going to give you three questions to ask yourself when determining: "Should I take this leap?"

I really pray this is helpful, biblical, and practical. I don't want to ignore your anxiety about the future, but I do want to help resolve it.

You can't wait forever. At some point you have to take action. So we're going to look at Peter's life in the book of Acts. Which, by the way, did you catch the name of the book we're looking at? *Acts.* This book records what the early church did while waiting for Jesus to return. Hence, the book is titled "Acts," not "Waits." A book titled "Waits" would be super boring. The wait is *active.* So let me show you three actions you can take while waiting for answers.

Setting the Scene

As we drop into Peter's life, we have to understand the social climate of the day. Peter is a major leader in the church, just as Jesus called him to be. However, Peter and the rest of the church are under intense persecution. It's not like people are merely being rude to Jesus followers. They were imprisoning and murdering them. Imagine your head being chopped off for believing in Christ. Imagine being set on fire as "entertainment" for the higher-up government officials. Sounds horrible right? Well that is what some of our earliest brothers and sisters in Christ went through.

While We Wait

In Acts chapter 12, Peter is in jail. He has no answers on what will happen to him. I'm sure he was curious. Wouldn't you be? Further, the church is worried too. They miss their leader. They're waiting to find out what's going to happen to Peter. Waiting on *someone else* is a whole different dimension of this "waiting" thing. Talk about feeling out of control. Yet, in the midst of this horrible season of waiting for answers, the church and Peter do three things that we can learn from and seek to do as well:

1. Uncommon Prayer
2. Common Obedience
3. Continual Persistence

As simple as they may be, the best question to ask yourself as you read this chapter is: *Am I doing these things?*

Simple ≠ Easy

Let me try to prepare the soil of your heart before you read this. Here is the painful truth: *Just because something is simple, doesn't mean it's easy.* Don't confuse the two. Is it simple to go to the gym five times a week? Sure. Is it easy? Nope. Now spiritually speaking, is it simple to cultivate disciplines of prayer and Bible reading? Is it simple to love your enemies? Is it simple to speak words of life rather than divisiveness? Yes, yes, and yes. Is it easy? Nope, nope, and nope.

Peter and the church do incredibly *simple* but *difficult* things while waiting for life-altering answers. They are things we must do while we wait. And let me be clear, they're not vague. You will be able to know very quickly if you are acting these things out. With that said, let's get to Peter's story and look at these actions.

1. Uncommon Prayer

Acts 12:5 (NIV) says, *"So Peter was kept in prison, but the church was* ***earnestly praying*** *to God for him."* I know what you're thinking, *Okay, the church was praying...so what? I'd be praying too if my friend was in jail.* I hear you. However, to understand why this is so powerful you can't just read verse 5, you have to read the start of the chapter as well. Acts 12:1-2:

> It was about this time that King Herod arrested some who belonged to the ***church***, intending to persecute them. He had ***James***, the brother of John, put to ***death*** with the sword.

You know why the church's prayer for Peter impresses me? Because James was just put to death in jail. It's one thing to pray for Peter. It's another thing to pray for Peter *after* James was just in the exact same situation and was murdered.

You don't think the church was praying for James too? You don't think they cried out to God saying, "Oh, Lord! He's doing Your will. Protect him!" You don't think the church even prayed prayers they saw in the Psalms about God delivering them from the presence of their enemies? Of course they did all those things! And what happened?

James died. God answered their prayer with an answer they didn't want. And what happened? They kept. On. Praying. And not little timid prayers. The Bible says they prayed *earnestly*.

That word *earnestly* means "fervently and constantly."[1] It's the same Greek word used to describe Jesus' prayer in Luke 22:44. You remember that prayer? That's the one when Jesus prayed so earnestly that drops of blood fell as sweat. The prayer that gave Him the strength to die on a cross, descend to hell, and still utter the words, *"Not My will but Yours be done."* Yeah, that's the kind of "earnest" prayer I'm talking about. That prayer is uncommon.

It's very common for people to roll out of bed without praying at all. It's even more common for people to give 15 minutes a morning that's half devoted to the Bible on their phone and half devoted to the random notifications that pop up while reading. It's also common for people to worry out loud to God and label it a prayer.

I think it's uncommon to put the distractions away, get the Word out, pray with conviction, and encounter heaven until we're changed on the inside. I'm talking about the type of encounter that reminds you prayer isn't about getting God to do your will in heaven, it's about Him getting you to do His will on earth. It's that kind of prayer where you somehow, by God's grace, find the strength to utter, "not my will but Yours be done." *That's* the kind of prayer the early church was praying, even in the midst of disappointment.

I'm inspired by the church's earnest prayer, because I'm not sure I would have kept praying earnestly. Would I have prayed earnestly for James? Yeah! For Peter? I don't know. Earnest prayer after disappointing answers is tough. But the church didn't let anything negative grow in the middle of unanswered prayer.

We have to be so careful about what grows in the middle of unanswered prayer. What happened to you when God didn't answer your prayer about your parents staying together? What happened to you when God didn't answer your prayer for healing like you thought He should? What happened to you when God didn't answer your prayer about getting into the school you wanted, finding the relationship you thought was perfect, or bringing your kid back to Him yet? It's easy to pray for James. It's hard to pray for Peter.

Pay attention to what grows in the middle of unanswered prayers. Some of us get more cynical toward God. "Yeah, He works for some people I guess, but not me." Some of us get angry. "He doesn't care about me." But I love this church in Acts—even though God didn't answer their prayer about James as they thought He would, they're still earnestly praying while waiting on an answer regarding Peter. It's like the devil took his best shot, and they kept fighting. What can the devil do with someone who has faith like that?

You may be waiting. You may even be disappointed in your wait. The following is an action every one of us can take before we get our answer (or when we get an answer we don't like):

Actions to Take Before Answers Arrive

Don't Mess with Mama or Grandmama

I've been blessed to have *uncommon prayer* modeled to me. My mom is a praying machine. I can't tell you the amount of times I was just trying to go to first grade and couldn't get out of the car without a loud plea for angels to "guide, guard, protect, and direct" me. I don't care how tired we were, we weren't going to bed without Mom praying for us. One time, I was doing something *really dumb*—like "easily could have killed me" dumb—at 2 a.m. My mom texted me at 2 a.m., "Hey G, praying for you. I feel like God's telling me you're doing something dumb." She's the type of mom who would fake going to the bathroom to get away from four little tornado children so she could get a quick prayer in. And if I went to her closet and it was shut, the gates of heaven weren't. She had that *uncommon* prayer.

Her mom was an uncommon pray-er, too. My grandma is kind of a big deal. Her name is Dodie Osteen. More than 40 years ago, she was diagnosed with cancer. She was given three weeks to live. You know what she did? Prayed. And prayed. And prayed. Each time she went back to the doctor, she was expecting a good report. But each time, she got a worse one. Did that stop her? Nope. She prayed and prayed and prayed. One day, feeling hopeless, she took out her Bible and stood on it. She cried, "Lord, I don't know what else to do. So I am literally standing on Your Word." She was given three weeks to live.

Well, I don't know if you noticed, but she wrote the Foreword for this book. You know what that means? She lived a lot more life than the doctors thought. Now, *that's* the part that most people celebrate. And no doubt, we should celebrate that! But when I tell the story, I tell it a little bit differently.

My grandfather was a great man of God. He frequently prayed over the sick and saw them healed. I'm proudly named after him! (My name is JOHN Geoffrey Graff). Guess what? In 1999, he was diagnosed with congestive heart failure. Guess what he did? Prayed. And prayed. And prayed. Did he have faith? Absolutely! A large part of his life was dedicated to healing the sick! And guess what happened? He passed away that year.

My Grandmama passed away a couple weeks after the finishing of this book (right after she wrote the foreword to it)! You know what she did until her dying day, at 91 years old? She prayed for the sick. Sometimes she prayed in a little room at the church. Sometimes she prayed in the parking lot as people pulled up in her "drive-through prayer line." Yeah, you read that right. Most people have drive-through lines for burgers. Grandmama had a drive-through line for prayer. Spiritually speaking, she was cold-blooded. And that's why I have so much respect for her. While waiting for answers and even after receiving answers she didn't like, she would not quit praying.

The Church, My Grandmama, and You

It's easy to pray for James. It's hard to pray for Peter. It's easy to pray when God heals you of cancer. It's hard to pray when He lets your husband die of congestive heart failure. But *for uncommon prayer warriors, the answer is less important than the encounter.* What do I mean? Prayer is about that encounter with heaven that helps you accept what God gives and trust it's for your best. Is it simple? Yes. Is it easy? No.

Uncommon prayer is the type of prayer that simply will not quit—because it knows that the God listening won't quit. He may not have done everything you expected, but He's working out something greater for your good and His glory. His will is always perfect and good, and it's always more understood in retrospect.

I know you're waiting, but have you quit praying? I mean *earnestly* praying. I mean that type of prayer that isn't half-hearted because the other half of the heart is watching TV. I mean that type of *desperate* prayer that feels nothing, but you don't quit. Instead, you study the Bible and other trusted resources on how to pray and you keep showing up to talk to God. I mean that type of prayer that realizes we must pray as if our life depends on it, because it does depend on it.

I'm going to talk to you how I talk to myself, and it's only because I care about you. It's time to get off your butt and get on your knees. God has a vision for your life. It's not easy. Do you really believe apart from Jesus you can do nothing? If so, you pray. There will be valleys and mountains. Your life will involve picking up your cross. But the only way you will be fulfilled is to pick up that cross. And the only way you'll have the power to pick it up is through the earnest prayer that ultimately ends in the most heartfelt, "not my will, but Yours be done."

You can only truly mean those words after encountering God in prayer and being gripped by His loving Spirit. If you're not praying like that, don't expect to get through this waiting season well. What an example we have from the early church. Now let's look at Peter, because *uncommon prayer is always met with common obedience.*

2. Common Obedience

While the church is praying, Peter is waiting. Then Acts 12:7-8 (NIV) happens:

> Suddenly an angel of the Lord appeared and a light shone in the cell. He struck Peter on the side and woke him up. "Quick, ***get up***!" he said, and the chains fell off Peter's wrists. Then the angel said to him, "Put on your ***clothes*** and sandals." And Peter did so. "Wrap your cloak around you and ***follow me***," the angel told him.

Can you imagine that? Getting struck on the side by an angel who is breaking you out of jail? What a wild night. Yet in this wildness, there is wisdom.

The angel tells Peter to get up and get dressed. It makes me laugh because he just miraculously appeared in the prison cell and snapped the chains. Why doesn't the angel just put Peter's clothes on the same way he took Peter's chains off? But he breaks chains and tells Peter, "Get dressed." It reminds me, *God always gives us a common part to play in the uncommon miracles we ask for.* If you're in a waiting season here's another action to take:

Actions to Take Before Answers Arrive

Time and time again in the Bible we see this is Jesus' M.O. Remember when He raised Lazarus from the dead? Although Jesus could move the stone Himself supernaturally, rather, He told someone to move the stone away (John 11:39). If you can raise a dead body, surely you can move a stone. But the people had a common part to play. Remember when Jesus fed the 5,000? He blessed the food and then gave the loaves to the disciples to distribute (Matthew 14:19). Why not just multiply it by making it appear to the people where they were? Or why not do the "manna from heaven" thing again and make it rain food? Because the people had a common part to play.

Now, let's go back to Peter's prison break. After this incredible miracle of an angel teleporting into the jail and snapping chains apart, Peter and the angel are about to commonly sneak past two guards and go through the city gate. Why? Why not just teleport *out of* the city like the angel teleported *into* the jail? Who knows. What we do know is that Peter had a common part to play. He was to get up, get dressed, and follow.

I'm doing some imagining here, but don't you think Peter would have been a little bit afraid to sneak past the two guards? And even if he got past the two guards, don't you think he would have been worried about the huge iron gate guarding the city? Who was going to open that thing? Wouldn't the guards hear it open and capture him? Yet, Peter obeys with something as simple as getting up, getting dressed, and following.

And here's the humor of the story. As they got closer to the gate, a miracle happened: The gate *"opened for them by itself"* (Acts 12:10 NIV)! It was like one of those motion-activated gates. You know, the ones that open, but *its opening* is contingent on *your moving* toward it.

This is a great visual for how acting in common obedience works with God acting in miraculous ways. We can sit there, look at a closed gate, and say, "God, open it." And He says, "I already told you to go." And we'll be like, "I'll go when You open it." And He says, "No. *You have to go toward it so it will open. You have to make the move."* What if God wants to do a miracle in your life but it's contingent on you moving? In the passage, we see uncommon prayer *and* common obedience. I don't think that's an accident.

Are you being obedient to something *common* God asked you to do? I truly believe if you have uncommon prayer and common obedience, God will open what needs to be opened. If you have uncommon prayer and common obedience, He will move what you can't move. Please never underestimate the power of obeying the seemingly insignificant common things that you know to do, even in the absence of answers you're still waiting for. God shows Peter, "I'll break chains and open gates. You get dressed and start moving before I do it!"

I can't help but wonder how many believers are waiting on God to do an incredible miracle, but He's waiting on us to show common obedience. Are you praying for something big, but unwilling to do something little? Are you praying for reconciliation, but unwilling to go to counseling? Are you praying for a job, but unwilling to live with the discipline to build a good resume? Are you praying for forgiveness, but unwilling to ask for it? Are you praying for a Christian community, but unwilling to get involved at your church? Are you praying for provision, but unwilling to make a budget?

I know you're waiting, but the wait is *active*. I know there are roadblocks, but those often move out of the way as you get moving. God will break chains, but you get dressed. God will open gates, but you get moving. In the wait, you can always pray, and you can always do the common things God has asked of you. And then guess what? You keep. On. Doing it. In this passage, *uncommon prayer* is matched with *common obedience,* but they are both matched with *continual persistence.*

3. Continual Persistence

Persistence is key in life, and it's key in this passage. Let me show you how. Peter gets out of jail, but he's not sure where to go. He ends up going to the house where everyone is praying for him (probably a good call). The Bible says in Acts 12:13–16 (NIV):

> Peter knocked at the outer entrance, and a servant named Rhoda came to answer the door. When she recognized Peter's voice, she was so overjoyed she ran back without opening it and exclaimed, "Peter is at the door!" "You're out of your mind," they told her. When she ***kept insisting*** that it was so, they said, "It must be his angel." But Peter ***kept on knocking***, and when they opened the door and saw him, they were astonished.

What does this have to do with persistence? Every character had a part to play in this story that involved persistence. I am a huge fan of reading the Bible slowly, so let me just break it down for you like this:

- The church *kept praying* (verse 5)
- The servant *kept insisting* (verse 15)
- Peter *kept knocking* (verse 16)

We need consistent prayer and we need common obedience. But even in the midst of those things, we need continual persistence.

I know waiting is hard. And if you're like me, it can throw you into a state of paralysis. When you aren't doing what you feel called to do, it can be easiest to do nothing at all. Is God ever going to answer your prayers? Yes. Sometimes in a way you like, sometimes in a way you don't like. But I don't care who you are, while you're waiting for answers this story reminds us you can still take these actions.

Actions to Take Before Answers Arrive

1. Uncommon Prayer
2. Common Obedience
3. Continual Persistence

Are these actions simple? Yes. Are they easy? No. But the simple, faithful actions are what shake heaven. Why? Because faith gets the attention of God, and *the greatest proof of your faith is your faithfulness.*

Keep on going, because your faithfulness shows your faith. God will take off the chains (Acts 12:7) but tell you to put on your clothes (verse 8). He will open the iron gate without effort when you walk toward it (verse 10). God wants to see if you have enough faith to keep knocking at the door that should easily open at your friend's house (verse 16). He's the God of incredible miracles, but He always gives you a part to play.

So in your wait, keep *acting* on what you know to do. Don't quit just because it gets hard. Don't quit because it's not convenient. Don't quit because you didn't see the results you wanted as quickly as you wanted. And for sure, don't quit because you don't have the "clarity" you need. Maybe you need less clarity than you think. Often, action must come before answers.

But What About Uncommon Obedience

I do understand there are certain decisions that are bigger than "common obedience." There are some decisions in life that are huge leaps of faith. Those leaps are risky and sacrificial. They're not lesser decisions such as, "Should I volunteer at church?" Or, "Should I apply for this job while in college?" Those really aren't that big of a deal. I'm talking about decisions that cause you to sacrifice a lot. Those, "Abraham leave everything you know" type of decisions. The decisions that could affect the rest of your life and affect those around you. These type of decisions include: who to marry; what should be your college major; should you start a business and quit your job; should you uproot everyone and move to a different location, taking your family from its current support system. I want to address *those* decisions before moving on to the next chapter.

For instance, my decision to leave the security of where I was and plant a church from scratch wasn't a common, everyday decision. I did not make the decision quickly. My pregnant wife and I moved across the country with no promise of a job. And guess what? When we did it, I still didn't have 100 percent clarity that I should. It was scary!

I went on a prayer and fasting retreat and turned to some books written by early church fathers for some guidance (in addition to my main source, the Bible, of course). My decision-making process was drastically altered by some advice given by Saint Ignatius of Loyola. It is recorded in a book titled *Discerning the Will of God* by Timothy Gallagher.[2]

Wisdom from Ignatius

Essentially, Ignatius notes that there are times when you are faced with uncommon decisions and simply can't discern which choice is best to make. God isn't giving total clarity, and it's frustrating. Besides, our emotions are so wrapped up in the decision that it can be hard to think straight. When faced with times like this, Ignatius would ask himself three questions. These questions helped me *act* and not waste the wait.

The first question: "What advice would I give a total stranger in my same situation?"[3] As funny as it sounds, this can be extremely helpful. Sometimes, it's a little bit harder to see the situation clearly when we are the one who is in it. If you were advising a total stranger rather than being the person going through the decision-making process, the same feelings of fear, disappointing others, failure, etc., are less amplified, which can make it easier to see the situation clearly. However, if that still doesn't work, Ignatius asks another question.

The second question Ignatius asks is, "What choice would I be most proud of making on my deathbed?"[4] For me, this was incredibly helpful to ask myself. It forced me to wrestle with what I felt a *responsibility* for. I knew that if I lay on my deathbed not having stepped out in faith to plant a church, I would have always regretted it. I also realized, on my deathbed, I'll care about how I loved my family and friends more than anything. This decision of whether or not to plant a church didn't necessarily affect how I would be able to love them. Again, this question helped me clarify what mattered most to me. Last, if you still don't have a sense of whether or not you should take a leap of uncommon obedience, Ignatius moves to his third question.

The third question is, "What choice will I be most happy I made when facing Jesus on judgment day?"[5] Somehow I had never thought to ask myself this question. Once I wrestled with and prayed through this question, I came to a realization: Whatever decision I made would be made from a heart desiring to please Jesus. At the end of the day, whether I made the right or wrong decision, knowing I truly aimed to please Jesus was enough for me.

Conclusion: You Need Less Clarity

As I close this chapter, please know that God rarely gives you the clarity you want. In fact, *God will never give you so much clarity that you no longer need to trust Him*. I know you want answers, but often action comes before answers. Ask Abraham, who had to go to a land before God showed him which land. Ask Peter, who had to sneak past the guards before he knew how the city gate would open. The biblical pattern isn't one of immense clarity. It's one of immense trust in God.

The Bible doesn't command us to know everything before we make a decision to act. It commands us to know God so well that we have the faith to act. *Action* shows faith. And yet, if you take action, you'll get answers. *That's* what I see in the Bible. So what are you waiting for? The wait is active.

5 ACT WITHOUT COMPARISON

Have you ever had a moment of intense comparison? I don't mean those little bouts of comparing yourself with some super strong guy in the gym and think, *Man, I don't look like that,* then resume your day. I mean those times when you compare to the point it literally makes you feel like giving up or not trying at all. Maybe you want to start a podcast but have 30 followers compared to other people's thousands of followers. The only thing worse than no comments is a single comment from your mom or grandmother ("This was so good, Sweetie!"). Let's just not start the podcast, right?

Or maybe you want to pursue a business venture but compared to other businesspeople's experience, you have no business doing so. Maybe you'll just keep your current job instead, right? Or maybe it's something as simple as serving in a small group, but compared to Linda who is 98 years old and somehow has 100 years of experience, who would listen to you? You'll just keep being a greeter, right? Here's what I'm saying: *One of the biggest reasons we don't act is because we compare ourselves to others.* We have to get rid of a comparison mindset.

MY FIRST BIG STRUGGLE WITH COMPARISON

I started preaching at 15 years old to fifth and sixth graders at my home church. I would study up on the curriculum, and I would not tell anyone in my family I was preaching the next day. Worse than having no one listening is having *only* your mom listening. Not to mention mom's obligatory Facebook post of my acne-ridden self, sleeping fifth graders, and a caption that reads something cheesy like, "World changer!" Thanks, Mom.

Regardless I kept preaching, and I actually started studying and preparing my own messages at 17. As I got into my early 20s, I traveled in the United States preaching at summer camps, preaching in my college classes, and occasionally preaching at other youth groups. I was decent but had a lot more confidence than skill.

When I was 20 years old I had preached for my home church's youth camp. Eleven years later, I could still tell you exactly what I preached on. I thought I really nailed it. Until this other young youth pastor named Cody preached.

I normally won't name-drop unless it's a good example, and let me tell you, Cody could *preach*. I have no idea where he is these days. I doubt he'll ever read this, and I don't even remember his last name. But to the Cody who preached at Ignite Summer Camp in Palacios, Texas, I hope you're doing well!

I remember sitting there thinking, *These kids are getting the Word of God and they are* ***engaged***. Not only that, but the revelation and conviction Cody brought was so good! Surely, me being a preacher, I would rejoice at the gift of this talented preacher, right? Wrong. The enemy is so tricky. When I should have been celebrating, I was comparing. I thought, *Maybe I'm not that good. Maybe I should change my major. Maybe I'll be an architect like the original plan.*

Comparison was the reason I almost quit acting on what God was calling me to do.

These days, I am a lot more aware of my tendency to compare, but just because I am aware doesn't mean the enemy stopped trying to make me do it. The other day I was preaching at a conference. They were announcing the lineup of speakers. About me, the host said, "We got Geoffrey Graff. He's one of the funniest preachers I know!" Okay, I'll take the compliment. Until the next speaker was announced as "one of the most anointed speakers" he knew. I sat there thinking, "What!?" The comparison trap was coming for me again, but I got out of it pretty quickly. I hope to help you get out of it, too.

The Double-Edged Sword of Comparison

The comparison trap has two sides, by the way. *Comparison either makes you feel inferior or superior—and neither of those are God's will for your life.* Think about it, the only way you feel inferior or superior is through comparison. All of us are prone to struggle with both sides of this double-edged sword. Maybe you don't think you struggle with comparison because you never feel *inferior*. I'm glad. But do you ever feel *superior*? If so, you struggle with comparison.

In this chapter, we talk mostly about the inferior side of comparison. But make no mistake, if you struggle with the superior side, you still need to give this a read. Because feeling superior is a sign you still haven't conquered comparison. And if you find fulfillment in feeling superior, one day someone will come along more gifted, more talented, with a bigger following, with more money.... By the world's standard, they will be "better" than you. If you haven't conquered comparison on the superior side, when you're on the inferior side, it will eat you alive.

I'm happy to share my immaturity and the ugliness of my heart with you. Why? Because I am not impressive at all. For me to act like I never have hang-ups would only divert glory that belongs to God for His ability to meet each and every one of us where we are and help us deal with the hurts that cause sin in our life. God's helped me a ton in this area. He is still helping me. I know he can help you, too.

And maybe, since "the funniest preacher" (eye roll) was honest with you, you can find a way to be honest with yourself. I'm not the only one who has struggled or will struggle with this; the enemy will try to get you to compare yourself, too. And if he can get you to compare, he'll eventually get you to quit. We can't waste the wait. We need to get rid of comparison.

The Parable of the Three Servants

Jesus tells a parable in Matthew 25 that confused me for the longest time. If you don't know, a "parable" is simply an earthly story with a heavenly meaning. In this parable, the master of a house goes away on a trip. But before he leaves, he calls three of his servants together. To the first he gives five bags of silver, based on his abilities. To the second he gives two bags of silver, based on his abilities. Last, to the third servant, he gives one bag of silver, based on his abilities. Then, the master leaves and the servants aren't sure when he'll return.

Eventually, the master returns and wants to know what the servants did with what they were entrusted. The first servant doubled his five bags and earned five more. The master was so proud of him that he entrusted him with even more responsibilities. The second servant also doubled his two bags and earned two more. Again, the master was so proud of him that he entrusted him with even more responsibilities.

However, the servant with one bag believed the master to be a harsh man. So he kept the money *safe*. He returned the one bag, having gained nothing and having lost nothing. The master called him "wicked and lazy," throwing him into outer darkness. For the sake of this chapter, I'm not going to wring this passage out for all it's worth (which I love trying to do). I'm going to talk about what's necessary for our topic of comparison.

Here's the general meaning of the parable: Jesus is the "master" on a trip who will come back at a "mysterious time." The "mysterious time" is simply the time Jesus will return from heaven to judge the world. None of us know when that will be. In the meantime, we are the servants entrusted with gifts from His hand. We are all given different gifts in different proportions. We are able to receive more or less depending on our faithfulness to develop what we have been given.

Our job is to be faithful with what God gives us, multiply it for the good of His house (aka His kingdom), and hear Him say, "Well done, My good and faithful servant." Pretty simple, right? But man oh man, is there a lesson about comparison in here that we could all benefit from. Let's talk about it.

Faithful Over First

I couldn't help but notice at the start of the story, one of the servants only received one bag of silver. I don't think it's a coincidence that this man was the one who didn't do anything with it. Right?

When I put myself in this guy's shoes, it's natural to start comparing! If you're the guy who received one bag, in your head you might think, *This is embarrassing. I got one bag, and everyone else has more. What does it matter what I do with this one bag? Even if I double it, I still won't have as much as the other guys.* In our own way, don't we think like this too? We look at our life and where we are, compare it to others, and if we feel inferior, then we choose to do nothing with it.

This mindset is normal. You know why? Because our culture puts greater emphasis on being first, not being faithful. In this chapter, I only want to share one big idea: ***to kill comparison thinking, think faithful, not first.***

If you're competitive like me, I know what you're thinking: *Who cares about faithfulness, I want to be first.* As the (false) prophet Ricky Bobby said, "If you're not first, you're last."

Here's the part of the scripture that shook me, though. When the master talked to the first servant who doubled his five bags to make ten, it says in Matthew 25:21 (NLT):

> The master was full of praise. "Well done, my good and faithful servant. You have been faithful in handling this small amount, so now I will give you many more responsibilities. Let's celebrate together!"

That servant earned more than everyone else; he was "first." So what's surprising about the master's response? That's how he should have responded, right? Except, look at how he responds to the "second place" guy who doubled his two bags to make four bags. Matthew 25:23 (NLT):

> The master said, "Well done, my good and faithful servant. You have been faithful in handling this small amount, so now I will give you many more responsibilities. Let's celebrate together!"

Did you catch it? To the guy who had ten bags (first place) and to the guy who had only four bags (second place) the master had the *exact same response.* Why? Because in God's eyes it's not about first, it's about faithfulness!

We are so prone to compare what we have to what other people have. We think, *It's a fraction of what other people have to offer. Who cares what I do with this?* And yet the resounding answer of this passage is: "God cares!" That's one of the main points of the story!

God doesn't judge how well you're doing based on the gifts He gave other people.

God didn't care about who was first, He cared about who was faithful. And He is the same today.

But if the enemy can get you to compare, he can get you to quit. *Who cares what vacation I take my kids on this year? It's not going to be at Disney like the neighbors.* God cares! Do something fun with the budget He gave you and teach your kids there's more to life than money! *Who cares how hard I study for that sermon for 20 kids? It's not like it's a Passion Conference.* God cares! So come prayed up and preach as if it was a Passion Conference, because that sermon may stick with one of those kids for the rest of their life!

No one person is so talented that the rest of us are allowed to stop doing our part. No one person is so anointed that they can love your family better than you, love their congregation better than you, love their friend group better than you. Actually, one Person *was and is* that important—His name is Jesus. He left earth and sent His Spirit because He knew we would be better off to have His Spirit enable us do our part than for Him to stick around. Yet, you may be sitting on the sidelines or doing things half-heartedly because by comparison, you don't feel important. *You are important! ACT like it.*

Just a Cog in the Wheel

My mom used to tell me something very simple and very deep. She would talk about life as if it was a big ol' machine. Which is funny because she is not mechanical at all. She struggles to put the TV on HDMI 1. In any case, she would talk about how in machines, there are all these gears connected to each other. Some are bigger, some are smaller, but they're all connected. As one turns, it turns the next, and the next, and the next. She would tell me, "You know G, we're all just cogs in the wheel. Gears in the machine. I'm not that big of a cog, but if I don't turn, the people around me won't turn. And that's true of you too."

That is the perfect perspective. It doesn't allow us to view ourselves as inferior or superior. It's a self-view that isn't filtered through comparison. When we see ourselves this way, we are faithful to "spin" in the "machine of God's kingdom," but we don't do it because we are trying to be better or because we think we are worse. We do it because we know we are important to the people around us. Do you see? Your world needs what you have to offer. More importantly, God cares what you have to offer, and He wants to celebrate it with you.

Do you see how freeing this mindset is? It helps you see yourself, not as inferior or superior, but as *important.*

God's Scale Is Different

As I close this chapter, I want to draw your attention to one more detail of the scripture. Did you notice how, to both the guy with five bags and the guy with two bags, God says, *"You have been faithful in handling this **small** amount…"* (Matthew 25:21,23 NLT). As the reader, we thought the five bags was a large amount, especially compared to the other two. But to God, they were all small amounts. Why do I bring this up?

The passage helps us keep our gifts in perspective. Whether you feel like you're a "one-bag person" or a "five-bag person," to God, what we have to offer is small. However, He still asks us to use it and longs to celebrate it. You know why? Because *something can be small and significant at the same time.* Don't believe me? Then explain ants, mosquitos, and fleas. I rest my case.

No matter who we are, God sees our contribution to His kingdom as very small and very significant. He wants us to see it the same way. God's not sitting up there blown away by the "greatest five-bag super Christians" of the world. Let's pretend the church I pastor grew to 25,000 people. That would be a *huge* church today. In the grand scheme of God's plan to save the world, 25,000 is pretty minor. In fact, I'd probably be forgotten in less than 100 years. My point is this: No matter who we are or what we do, our contribution is small and significant at the same time. The smallness should keep us humble. The significance should keep us confident.

You know who is going to hear, "Well done, My good and faithful servant"? The single parents who do everything they can to model a godly life under all the stress. The parents who stayed together and modeled a godly marriage. The people who aren't afraid to pray for someone at school or at work. The kid who owns his faith at school. The grandmothers whose faith spread to the family. The pastor who showed up to preach, love people, die, and be forgotten. God celebrates faithfulness, not first. We should celebrate that, too. But, where do we start?

Since I'm trying to get you to *act* in this section, I'm trying to also give you practical steps you can take. I ended the last chapter with practical questions you could ask, and I will end this one with a practical exercise you can do.

SOME PRACTICAL ADVICE

It can be daunting to know what God has given us and what He expects of us. So here's what I want you to do. Draw a Venn diagram with three circles.

In one circle write: "Best At." This circle represents the things that you are naturally best at. It doesn't mean you are better than everyone else. But when it comes to you, these things come easily. It could be math, hospitality, making people laugh. Whatever it is, you just know it's your natural gift. You don't even have to try that hard.

In the second circle, write: "Passionate About." This circle represents things you love. You can't explain it, but something in you comes alive when doing it. When you do these things, it's like time flies. An hour feels like a minute.

Okay, in the third circle, write: "Resources For." This circle represents what you actually have the resources to do. For example, maybe you've always wanted to be a pilot. Odds are, you don't have

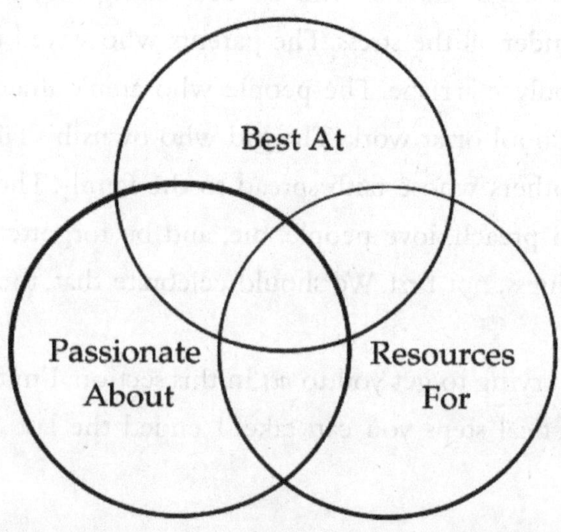

the resources to buy a plane. (If you do, please donate to Overflow Church. Just kidding. Kind of). But you probably do have the resources to enroll in a class to work toward earning your pilot license. Does it make sense?

Now, after you have completed all three circles, your job is to figure out what things fit every criteria. In other words, which things you are "best at," "passionate about," and have the "resources for."

I'll make myself an example so you can see how it works. I am "passionate about" golf, I even have "resources" (aka golf clubs), but man I am not "best at" it. So, it's a hobby. However, I am "best at" communicating, I am "passionate about" making the Word come alive to people, and God has blessed me with "resources" (a church) to express those gifts. That's why I am pastoring right now. You see?

Now for you, this will look completely different. You may be in high school. God made you best at sports, gave you a passion for them, and gave you the resources to place because you made the team. That very well may be what you should be doing with all your heart for His glory and to multiply His kingdom. You could be the athlete who doesn't cuss people out when they are angry and the one who knows your identity is greater than sports. As a matter of fact, God may be calling you to show your teammates that same thing. He might care about your attitude more than average points per game. But the gift, passion, and resource show the avenue He's asking you to use to multiply His kingdom.

Maybe you're a dad. You're "best at" connecting with kids, "passionate" about sports, and have the "resources" to coach the team. God very well may be calling you to coach that team and show the kids His love. It's not that complicated, you know?

Why did I tell you to pick those three categories? Because at the end of the day, you had *very little* to do with them. You didn't pick what you were naturally best at, God gave it to you. You didn't pick what you were passionate about, God made you like that. Last, in many ways the resources available to you aren't completely in your control either, these are a gift from God.

This is a simple but effective way to start using what God gave *right now* instead of wasting the wait. And guess what, as you use what you have, it begins to grow. Five bags become ten. Two bags become four. One bag becomes two. The only way it won't grow is if you bury it and do nothing with it because you think it's insignificant.

Summing Up

Unfortunately, so many of us waste the wait because of comparison. We look around, size ourselves up, and then decide what we have to offer is better buried than expressed. My friend, don't believe that lie. God could care less about how you stack up. Last I checked, at the end of the age we aren't going to be stacked up—we're going to be knelt down at the feet of Jesus. We'll be praising the only One who is worthy.

In the meantime, though, what will you do with what He gave you? When it comes to what you're best at, passionate about, and have the resources for, will you use it? God doesn't care if you're first. He cares if you're faithful. You're a cog in a wheel. If you don't spin, people around you won't. Carry humble confidence. What we offer is small, but it's significant. So get to work. Get active. Kill comparison by throwing off "first" and picking up "faithful." It's time to act.

6

ACT WITHOUT CONDEMNATION

The longer I've lived the more I've realized that everyone wants to do good. We may not all agree on what "good" means, but we all have a standard we hope to live by, and we feel shame if we break that standard. For Christians, that standard is God's Word, and disobeying it is what we call "sin." But again, everyone (Christian or not) hates to break their standard of goodness. Gang members don't want to be a "snitch." Parents who could care less about God still don't want to be seen as negligent. Athletes don't want to "crack under pressure." The world is full of people who hold many different beliefs regarding what's "good."Yet we share a common experience once that particular good is not achieved—shame.

Enneagram, Baseball, and Drums

I'm not sure if you're familiar with the *enneagram.* If not, don't worry about it. Some say it's demonic, some say it was founded by monks. I don't put too much stock in it, but I am an enneagram type "one." That means my core motivation is to be good.

Even since I was a kid, I was ultra-sensitive to doing bad, not even just morally. I was the kid who would strike out a couple times in a little league game and have to fight back the tears. I was the kid who would act tough when the coach yelled at me, but inside

I felt this gnawing agony and knew I had to work twice as hard to make it up.

I am also a drummer. I've played drums since I was 2 years old. It's my first language, though these days I don't play nearly as much as I wish I did. I remember one time, I was finally going to get to play for our youth summer camp. That was a *huge* deal. Granted, I was only going to play the morning service because I was on the "B team," but I was still on the team. I was ready. Or so I thought.

This was my big shot to be good and impress all of the "A team" (because that's what worship is about, right?). Well, I don't remember what happened except that I messed up, *big time*. It was so noticeable. It made the worship set so awkward. And my sixth grade, chubby, crooked-tooth self knew that I did *bad*.

Immediately after the worship set was over, I darted straight to the bathroom stall. I just sat there and cried, as if the world was over. My brother, who has the superpower of empathy, came in to check on me. He asked if I was okay. I replied, "Yeah bro, I'm all good." Then I whispered, "Is anyone else with you?" When he assured me he was alone, the tears broke loose. "This was my one shot, and I blew it! I completely ruined *Take It All*, now no one will get saved, and Brian, Justin, and Preston think I'm an idiot! I'm not playing the rest of camp."

At a young age, at the most elementary level, what was I experiencing? Shame. I did bad. But this is a very common human experience, no matter our age. As we grow up, we make mistakes. We don't just do little embarrassing things. We do things we aren't proud of that break God's standard for our life. We all feel shame, and shame can lead us to repentance or to condemnation.

Oftentimes, it leads us to condemnation: that feeling that there's no way out and the best thing to do is give up hope.

My story about the drums is silly, but as we grow up, the stories grow up with us. Maybe we experience shame for treating a friend badly. Instead of repenting and making things right, it's easier to hide from the friendship and let it drift off all together. Maybe we fail in our marriage. The shame can cause us to run somewhere else instead of staying and working things out. The principles and patterns are the same: We aren't good, we feel shame, we're tempted to run and hide rather than keep moving forward. When we stop moving forward, we waste the wait.

If we are not going to waste the wait and actually *act*, we need to get rid of condemnation.

So many people waste the wait, hiding because of their shame. They sit on the sidelines and ignore the plan God has for them, because they feel so much condemnation for the wrongs they've committed. It's a story as old as time.

Moses' Story

We see Moses doing this exact thing in Exodus 2–4. In this chapter, we look at Moses' story and explore three shame-based excuses we make that lead to condemnation and stagnation rather than acting by faith.

Moses has a complicated backstory. First off, he was born a Hebrew in a time period of mass genocide. The Pharaoh ordered all newly born Hebrew boys be killed. However, Moses' mother put him in a basket and sent him down the river. In addition to evading any sort of river-dwelling monster, Moses is found by Pharaoh's daughter. Surely, Moses would be killed, right? Wrong. Well, at least he would be enslaved like all the rest of the Hebrew people then, right? Wrong again. Moses, a Hebrew boy who should have been killed or enslaved, was taken in by the Pharaoh's daughter and he grew up in the Pharaoh's house.

What a weird situation to be born into. It had to be hard watching your people get beaten by the hands of Egyptians. It had to be even harder to get fed luxuriously in the palace by those same hands. All of this was hard on Moses.

One day, Moses went out to visit his own people. He saw how hard they were forced to work and how brutally they were treated. He had a desire to see them free and treated justly, so this infuriated him. It infuriated him so much that he acted rashly and killed the Egyptian who was harshly supervising the Hebrews, and then he buried the body.

The next day, someone called him out on it, and then it hit him—shame. What did he do? He ran away to the land of Midian, and he hid for 40 years. You probably know the story. In the next chapter of Exodus, God chases down Moses in Midian and calls him to lead the people out from Egyptian slavery. However, Moses' shame led to condemnation. And since he is under condemnation, he is having a hard time *acting* on what God is asking. Instead, he makes excuses for why he isn't good enough.

The Root of the Excuse

Before making his three excuses in Exodus 4, Moses and God have a little argument in Exodus 3. God tells Moses that he is called to lead the Israelites out of slavery. Moses didn't think he was the type of person God should use. After 40 years of hiding, he *still* has a shameful view of himself. How do I know? Because in Exodus 3:11 Moses protests by saying to God, *"**Who am I** to do this?"*

Don't miss this important point. Moses tried to waste the wait. He spent 40 years hiding and apparently wanted to keep hiding. Why? Because he couldn't get past *who he was*. It all tied back to his shame. Moses was letting the lowest moment of his life become his identity.

What about you? *We can't let one low moment become our identity.* If we let a certain instance become our identity, we waste the wait. We'll never act because we are stuck in shame.

My friend, I think you and I are similar to Moses. How much of our passiveness is fueled by the "Who am I" question that plagues us? We, like Moses, wear our mistakes as our identity and disqualify ourselves from the assignment God gave us. "Who am I to talk to my friends about Jesus? I was the one who was partying with them." "Who am I to give this couple marriage advice? My marriage was a wreck at their age too." "Who am I to try to get back into my kids' lives? I drove them away for years."

As a pastor, I've seen these shame-based excuses turn into condemnation that fuels a life of sitting on the sidelines. And guess what? Satan loves it.

Think with me, though. What is the story arc we find throughout the Bible? Perfect people being used by God? No. Was it people who had a past, then got saved, started following Jesus, and never messed up again? No! Did the apostle Peter stop ministering after committing apostasy as Jesus' disciple? No. A short time later he was restored to Jesus and led the church. Did David, a man after God's own heart, stop reigning as king after his murder and affair? No. He kept reigning and even asked God to restore the joy of his salvation so he could *"teach transgressors Your ways"* (Psalm 51:13 NKJV). Did Abraham stop following God after continually not trusting the plan, sleeping with his servant, and putting his wife in jeopardy time and time again? No! He went on to accomplish the call God had for him.

Here's the Bible's common thread: We are all sinners in need of the Savior. All of us can recall things we've done and think, "Who am I?" And while it is great to embrace humility, it's not great to embrace condemnation. In other words: *Shame can be useful if it's leading us to humility and repentance, but it's not meant to lead us to condemnation and passiveness.* God has more for you than that. Likewise, He had more for Moses than hiding out in shame for the remainder of his life. So let's look at Moses' three excuses in Exodus 4, and see if we can find ourselves anywhere in the story.

EXCUSES THAT KEEP US STUCK

1. THE ASSIGNMENT IS TOO HARD.

Moses' first excuse is in Exodus 4:1 (NLT) where he asks God, *"What if they won't believe me or listen to me?"* In other words, "God, even if I am willing, I can't control what they think! There is a lot that is out of my control here. I'm not sure I'm the guy for this job." Sound familiar?

We can look at what God's asking us to do and think, *There's too much not in my control. I'm not the person for the job, God.* Why? For the same reason as Moses. In the back of our mind, we are still wearing shame and thinking, *Who am I? I'm not good enough!* And from that mindset, it's easier to make this excuse—the assignment is too hard.

2. MY ABILITY IS INSUFFICIENT.

That's not where Moses' excuses stopped, though. After Moses tells God the job is too hard, he then says, *"O Lord, I'm not very good with words"* (Exodus 4:10 NLT). Excuse after excuse.

First Moses had a problem with the assignment, now he has a problem with his own ability. Have you ever felt like that? Of course you have. So have I. We all make this second excuse.

I don't think anyone ever feels completely able to do what God calls them to. Have you ever heard of the term "imposter syndrome"? It's basically the feeling someone gets that tells them, "You shouldn't be the one who's doing this. You're not able." Doctors get imposter syndrome, teachers get imposter syndrome, parents get imposter syndrome. Even pastors get it!

There is certainly a level of "readiness" we need as we step into what God is calling us to do or say. In fact, the whole next section is about improving our abilities.

However, shame can cause us to see ourselves as completely inadequate and unable, influencing us to do nothing and waste precious years. At the end of the day, Moses was one of the best leaders we see in the Bible, and he almost didn't lead the Israelites out of slavery because of this shame-based excuse.

3. ANYONE CAN DO IT.

Finally, Moses has one final protest. This was his last attempt to keep hiding and waste the wait. In Exodus 4:13 (NLT), Moses begs God by saying, *"Lord, please! Send anyone else."* In other words, Moses was saying, "Anyone can do this!"

Technically, Moses was right. God could have used anyone. However, God trusted Moses with this task. This is how we should think. Rather than an "anyone can do it" mindset, we should have a "God trusted me with this" mindset.

God trusted *you* with those kids. God trusted *you* with that elementary class. God trusted *you* with that spouse. God trusted *you* with that coworker. God trusted *you* to coach that team. God trusted *you* with that youth group. Could someone else do it? Sure. But God trusted *you*.

Don't let shame be the reason you don't do it. If we take the "anyone can do it" mindset, it's an excuse to not act. If we take the "God trusted me with this" mindset, it's a reason to act by faith.

Are you making any of these three excuses? Are you wasting the wait because of shame? Are you hesitant because you're thinking about the times you tried and failed? Are you thinking about the embarrassment you felt when you let people down?

The funny thing is, I'm not here to tell you, "You can do it! You're good enough!" While I do believe you can do it, I think that misses the whole point of God's encounter with Moses. The point of the encounter is *incredible*, but it's not about how good we are. If we can receive the message, though, we'll get out of shame and get back to acting by faith.

The Point of the Passage

Did you notice that I left out God's responses to Moses' three excuses? I was saving them for right now. Here is a concise, paraphrased version of every response God gives Moses.

Moses' Protests and God's Responses in Exodus

Moses: "Who am I…?"
God: "I will be with you." (Exodus 3:11-12)
Moses: "What if they don't listen or believe You're with me?"
God: "I'll do miracles for proof." (Exodus 4:1-9)
Moses: "I'm not good at speaking."
God: "Who makes the mouth speak?" (Exodus 4:10-12)
Moses: "Send anyone else!"
God: "Fine, I'll go with you and your brother." (Exodus 4:13-17)

Did you notice anything? Not *one time* did God answer Moses' doubts by bringing assurance of Moses' capabilities. That's what we like though, right? We love when someone encourages us by telling us how good we are! "Oh, you're a fantastic mom! You have so much empathy. You'll be fine." "Oh bro, you'll do fine! You are a hard worker!" That kind of assurance makes us feel good. And at times, those words are incredible and needed!

Yet, Moses didn't get the assurance that he was good enough. Instead, Moses got the assurance that *God* was good enough. *God* was capable of making it happen!

THE ONLY ANSWER TO SHAME THAT HELPS

I believe in you. I believe you have gifts, talents, and strengths to do what God is calling you to do. However, those are not the reasons you are going to be okay. You are going to be okay because *God* is in the picture. You are going to be okay because *His* grace is sufficient. You are going to be okay because *He* will go with you. You will look back on mistakes you made. Sins you committed. You will even make mistakes as you try your very best. And that's when it will hit you: His grace filled in the cracks and made up the shortcomings. His strength made up for the weakness you carried. His protection guarded you when you were most susceptible. His righteousness was enough even when you made mistakes you're ashamed of. His love gave you the power to forgive, move on, and step out in faith.

In short: God didn't put you in the game because you were "good enough," so He's not taking you out because you weren't good enough. We are "in the game" and have a part to play because of His goodness. God's grace both starts us and sustains us in this race we are running for Him.

Moses learned that his worst mistakes weren't more powerful than God's mercy and love. My friend, your shame is not more powerful than God's grace. So throw off that shame and keep pressing forward by God's grace. Don't let shame be a reason you sit on the sidelines and waste the wait.

I'm not a motivational speaker, I'm a preacher. I love to preach the gospel. But the gospel is not self-help, nor is it self-improvement. The gospel is self-abandonment. It's knowing, *"He must increase, but I must decrease"* (John 3:30 NKJV). Because, left to our own talents and capabilities, we are not enough. But with the grace of God and His Spirit inside us, watch out! We are powerful!

Though we may be like fragile jars, we have a special treasure inside us (2 Corinthians 4:7). We have the living God dwelling within. *That's* the reason we step out in faith and act. Not because we are perfect. Not because we are ready and won't trip along the way. We act because the hand of God is on our life, and though we may trip, He will not let us fall (Psalm 37:24).

God goes with you. He loves you. He believes in you. He died for you and called you, knowing every mistake you would *ever* make—not just the mistakes you made before you got saved. He sees your end from the beginning, and *He* is with you in all of it. That's why you'll be okay.

Breaking a Cycle of Shame

We can often be like Moses. Paralyzed in fear. Stuck in shame. Wasting the wait because of a bad past. Yet God comes on the scene to basically get one message across: *Moses, don't make your failures greater than My faithfulness.* He says the same thing to you and me. Please stop making your failures greater than His faithfulness. Don't cheapen what Jesus did on the Cross by acting like your failure is the exception that the grace of God doesn't cover. God loves you and is for you. Don't stay stuck in shame. Your guilt and shame has been paid for on the Cross; don't pay for it twice by wallowing in condemnation.

I heard a story about a dad, his son, and a fire. The story took place when people still rode horses. The dad and son woke up in the middle of the night and noticed that their house and pasture were on fire. The dad rushed to put his son on a horse. As they started to ride through the flames, the dad quickly turned around and rode to a spot where the fire already burned. He made his son get off the horse and stand there in that spot. The boy cried, "I don't want to stay here, Dad; it's scary! There's fire all around me!" The dad looked down and said, "I know, son. But this spot has already been burned. And as long as you're standing in this spot, it can't be burned again. It's scary, but stand in the spot that has already been burned. You'll be okay."

My friend, Jesus took the wrath of God and punishment for our sin. Jesus is the Spot that has already been burned. Will you stand in Him? Whenever the devil accuses you, will you stand in the Spot that has been burned and remind yourself, *"I have been crucified with Christ and I no longer live, but Christ lives in me. The life I now live in the body, I live by faith in the Son of God, who loved me and gave himself for me"* (Galatians 2:20 NIV). Would you run *to* Him, not *from* Him, and remember that, *"If we confess our sins, he is faithful and just to forgive us our sins and to cleanse us from all unrighteousness"* (1 John 1:9 NIV).

When I am stuck in ruts of condemnation, I often turn to 1 John 2 that talks about Jesus as our Advocate (Lawyer) who defends us before the Father (Judge) as the devil accuses us. This is the picture it paints: The devil is making his best case against you. He's pointing the finger at you and running your name and reputation through the dirt. The worst part is, he is right. He is saying stuff you really did do. Yet, after the devil makes his best case, Jesus yells out, "Objection!"

Then Jesus, our Lawyer, approaches the Judge. Looking at the Judge, Jesus says, "Hey, Dad. They are guilty. They have actually done much worse than what they're even being accused of. But they're not just guilty, they're also *Mine*. The penalty for their sins has been paid by My death on the Cross. You abandoned Me on the Cross. I absorbed every ounce of Your wrath, and was separated from You in hell. And when I did that, I did it with their sin in My mind and with love in My heart for them. So please, because You are a fair judge, don't make anyone pay for this sin twice. Release them into My loving care as we work through their sin together."

And the Father looks at the accuser, bangs the gavel and declares, "Innocent!" Satan throws a fit. He's reminded that he has no power. He's reminded that shame can't keep you on the sidelines. And guess what? It gives the Father great joy to see you get up and go on your way with a thankful heart. So get up and get on your way. Shame has worked too long in your life.

God knows exactly where you are, what you've done, and what He's calling you to do. Confess, repent, and walk to Him. The cool thing about God is when you walk to Him, He's already running to you. He has a smile on His face. He's ready to sweep you up, dust you off, and clothe you as His own.

Tell some trusted people what you're going through. If they're truly the people of God, they won't flinch at your sin. They'll embrace you, tell you they're sinners too, and help you find the *only* One who can help; the only One whose verdict of you means anything.

Many people think of their sin as a huge lake, separating them from God. We think, *If I can work through all this sin, I can get to God!* When Jesus came to earth and died for our sins, He did away with that model of us reaching God. We don't come to God. God came to *us*, even in our sin. And now, if you believe in your heart that Jesus is Lord and Savior, He stands beside you, with His arm around you, looking at your sin with you. Imagine Jesus smiling and saying, "I'm going to stick closer than a brother. Let's work through all this stuff together. I'm with you every step of the way." *That's* His heart toward those who call Him Lord.

Here's the point of Moses' story: God didn't come to Moses because Moses was finally good enough. God's not going to come to you because you're finally good enough, either. God comes to us because *He's* good enough. It's by *His* grace that He takes us and walks with us until little by little, inch by inch, we become more of the people He's calling us to be.

Don't let shame stagnate you. Don't let a low point define you. You failed? Get in line. I have too, in ways that break my heart and make me cringe. But guess what? Christianity is simply one beggar telling you where to find the bread. I'm a beggar, but I found the bread of life. His name is Jesus. When we are bad, He's still good. Your failure will *never* be greater than His faithfulness.

Some of us have been giving God the runaround like Moses: "The assignment is too hard, my ability's not enough, anybody can do this." But really, the root of our excuses is shame that drove us to hide in the first place. Please hear this: God doesn't just want anybody, He wants *you*! He's called you! He has so many important things for *you* to do.

He's waiting for you to take that step of obedience so He can meet you and help you when you can't help yourself! It's okay if you fail, He's faithful. It's okay if you missed it, that's what grace is for. Shame keeps you down, grace lifts you up and helps you follow Jesus again.

I'm harping on this because we're about to move on to the section of "improving." But let me be clear—it is grace that both *starts* and *sustains* us in our walk with Jesus. So, yes, we will improve. But we do not improve *to get grace*. We improve because grace has been given, grace won't be taken, and the rest of life is simply a way to say, "Thank You, Jesus. I want to give my best." So with a heart of gratefulness for the grace that we could never earn, let's shake condemnation and improve together.

SECTION THREE
IMPROVE

"God gives gifts like Ikea gives furniture. The pieces are there, but you have to put them together."

7
IMPROVE BY KILLING YOUR PRIDE

So, I have a confession: I love magic. Since I was little, I enjoyed being mesmerized by something as simple as the old "Is this your card?" trick. And don't get me started on something as complicated as making things vanish and reappear.

I think this stems from being left out as a kid. My brother, Mike, was into magic first. He went by "Magic Mike," but the name didn't age well (just kidding about that part). Mike would always choose my sister, Emily, to be his "assistant," and I had to be the "audience" who watched. That also meant I was the only one left out of knowing how the trick was pulled off.

So what did I do? I bought my own magic kits. You know—the fake thumb you can hide stuff in, the top hat you could pull stuff out of, the wand that turned into flowers. I had it all. I was obsessed with magic.

Truthfully, I never *completely* grew out of it. On our third wedding anniversary, I took Eden to a magic show (looking back, that was definitely a present to myself). I've sometimes wished God called me to be the guy that says, "Is this your card?" And when the person begins to say, "No," the person starts coughing, choking. Everyone is concerned for the person's health. I watch, mercilessly. Something begins to come out of their mouth. What is it? The Ace of Spades. Their card!

Everyone is in awe, I'm in my top hat smirking, and we are all mesmerized by magic. God had different plans for my life, though.

I say all this because the older I get, the more I see that God is in the business of miracles, but we often want a magic trick. What do I mean? Well, a *magic trick just does something* ***for*** *you. A miracle requires something* ***from*** *you, does something* ***in*** *you,* ***then*** *does something* ***for*** *you.* And the difference between those who experience the power of a miracle versus those who don't? Pride. Some theologians have said pride is the root of every sin ever committed. Pride is something we all struggle with. Nothing will cause you to stop improving like pride. Nothing will keep you stuck in your current state like pride. Nothing will cause you to waste the wait like pride. Ask Naaman.

Naaman's Background

Who in the world is Naaman? So glad you asked. Naaman was a military general in the Old Testament. He was one bad dude. He could command, he could fight, he could win. The Bible says he won victory after victory. However, he had something pretty scary going on—he was secretly suffering from leprosy (2 Kings 5).

Leprosy is a skin disease. It often starts small, but it can spread fast. It causes nerve damage and eventual loss of feeling to the affected part. It can weaken muscles to the point of uselessness. And it is *very* contagious. For this reason, lepers were often considered "unclean" and cast out of their communities. Ripped from their family and friends, lepers were left to die in their own leper colony unless some incredibly uncommon healing happened.

Why do I go into that much detail? Because now we can put ourselves in Naaman's shoes. Imagine being a country's "golden boy." People love you. You win for them. You keep them safe and are a threat to enemies. Now, all of that is at risk. If people knew what Naaman struggled with, he wouldn't be celebrated, he would be kicked out and left to die as if he never was a hero. So what does Naaman do? He hides his leprosy under his armor. *He hides his needs behind his strengths.* That's the thing about pride, though: pride uses our strengths to hide our needs.

Pride Uses Our Strengths to Hide Our Needs

To be honest, I have a lot of empathy for Naaman. We're all tempted to use our strengths to hide our needs. This problem occurs from a young age, and it continues to grow up in clever ways as we get older. I remember one particular kid in my youth group. His dad left his family when he was young; and as a result, the son walked around needing love and guidance.

Inside, it was so obvious that he was broken, insecure about life, and wanted a father figure. Who wouldn't? But that is a very humbling and vulnerable thing to admit, isn't it? So what did he do? He hid behind his exceptional athletic ability. He hid behind successful stat lines and scoreboard numbers. He acted like he could care less about his dad. He portrayed himself as the cool, confident person everyone wanted to be like. Why do this? Because if people could only see his strength, maybe they wouldn't recognize his needs. It's the same story of Naaman, thousands of years later.

I think of another grown man who did this too. He never had a father, and he struggled to be a good father. However, instead of admitting his weakness and need for help, he hid behind the impressive pay check he collected every two weeks. Why? Because if people can see his strengths, maybe they won't recognize his needs. But last time I checked, God didn't give His life for us because of our strengths. He gave His life for us because He loves us and knows our needs.

Strengths Covering Needs

When you're a mighty warrior like Naaman, it's easy to put the leprosy under the shining armor. People know how good you are with a sword in your hand, but not how limited you are because of a hidden need. It's easy for us to display what we're good at and hide where we need help. But we will never improve that way.

Now before we start throwing stones at Naaman, will you be open to the possibility that you do this too? I do it. I mean, I try not to. But it's instinctive to every human being. God frequently convicts me in areas of my life where He wants to develop me. At that point I have a choice: I can ignore it and hide my weaknesses behind my gifts, or I can confess to God and a few trusted people about my areas of weakness and ask God to transform me.

What about you? Are you being realistic in the areas of your life that you don't put on social media? I'm not saying display them to the world, that's unwise. I am saying, do you have needs you aren't scared to reveal to God and a few trusted people so that your strengths aren't covering your needs? If not, it's called pride. And it will keep you from improving the rest of your life.

A Spiritual Issue with Practical Outcomes

You can make this truth deeply spiritual, or insanely practical. It works either way. But it is always both. For example: Let's say you work a job you feel God called you to, and you love it. However, a coworker is better at the job than you are.

- *Humble* people won't feel threatened. They will be comfortable acknowledging how great that person is at the job, and they will seek to learn from them so they can improve and contribute at an even greater level.

- *Prideful* people will put down anyone who is better so they feel better about themselves. The result? They are more focused on people *thinking* they're good rather than actually getting better.

This points out a very interesting point: *much of our practical growth is contingent on our spiritual health.* Do you see? The prideful person won't improve at what God is calling them to because they won't listen to anyone or be transparent about their needs. So they are not growing at *practical skills*—but the root is a *spiritual issue.*

This is Naaman's case! Naaman could have cared less about his "spiritual health" and the pride in his heart. He merely wanted to get healed so he could get back to the battlefield and do his thing! In other words, he wanted a quick fix, not a deep work. He wanted a magic trick ("God, do this for me"), not a miracle ("God, do something inside that also changes me outside"). God loved Naaman way too much to heal his skin but not heal the inward sickness that was limiting him. God knew there was a deep, deep pride in Naaman's heart. His pride was what God wanted to take care of first. Here's how He did it.

Humble Pie

God put Naaman in some humbling situations to expose and heal his pride. You see, Naaman eventually told the king about his condition. He also told the king about a prophet in Israel (Elisha) who could potentially heal him. Obviously, Naaman is the king's "star player," if you will. The king was going to do everything in his power to help Naaman get healthy. So, the king loads up Naaman with a bunch of gifts and sends him on his way to Israel. Naaman was used to getting the best treatment, but he's going to experience "three strikes" that humble him and show his pride.

First, Naaman shows up to Israel with incredible gifts, and the king of Israel doesn't even go out to greet him. The king is intimidated because he knows he can't heal Naaman, so he just avoids him. Strike 1. Fortunately, the prophet Elisha tells the king to send Naaman to him. Yet, when Naaman gets to Elisha, Elisha doesn't even come out to meet him. Instead, Elisha sends a messenger to give Naaman orders. That's like Lebron James going to the doctor and then the receptionist comes out to say, "The doctor is too busy for you, but do these things." Yeah. Strike 2. However, it was what the messenger actually *said* to Naaman that was the biggest strike of all. It was "Strike 3"—the strike that broke Naaman and exposed his pride.

The messenger simply tells Naaman to go wash in the Jordan River (2 Kings 5:10). That's it. A quick wash and the leprosy would be gone. However, this made Naaman furious. He said, *"I expected him to wave his hand over the leprosy and call on the name of the Lord his God and heal me!"* (2 Kings 5:11 NLT).

Why would this make Naaman so angry? It seems like a pretty simple cure for *leprosy*, right? But here's the thing: the Jordan River was gross and dirty. No one wanted to go bathe in that water. It was humiliating. As simple as this was to cure his leprosy, Naaman thought it was "beneath him." You know what that means? He would never improve. Let's pause for a second and turn our attention to you. What do you consider beneath you?

WHAT'S "BENEATH YOU"?

Be careful what you consider "beneath you." Taking advice from smart people is not, beneath you. Admitting your weaknesses is not beneath you. Admitting that someone else (someone you might not even like) is better than you at something is not beneath you. Being a smart person at the table rather than the smartest person at the table is not beneath you. Pride will cause you to resist things that seem beneath you, and guess what? Just like Naaman, you will leave full of pride and with the same weakness you had, not improving one bit. When God calls you to the next thing, will you be ready? Nope. You'll waste the wait because of unchecked pride. I will too. No one is exempt from this.

At its root, pride convinces us we know better than God. Pride says that God's way is "beneath" our way. That's why pride is at the root of each sin we commit. Here, Naaman thought he knew better than God. He thought he knew how God should act, and because God didn't act in his way, Naaman wanted to leave.

Second Kings 5:11 clearly states that Naaman "expected" Elisha to wave his hand over the leprosy, call on his God, and heal him. There was an *expectation* on God that ended up being a *limitation* on Naaman. And that is another reason pride is so dangerous.

Pride Limits Expectations

Limiting Expectations

We often have a certain way we expect God to work. Here's what often happens when God doesn't meet our expectations: we get frustrated with Him, ignore His way, and stay stuck where we are. Wasting precious time that could be spent improving.

Let me give you an example I saw frequently as a youth pastor. I pastored high school students who were in dysfunctional relationships. Let's say, for example, there was some unchecked lust in their hearts. At some point, the relationship would turn south. The kids would come up to me and ask that God heal their dysfunctional relationship. That was *their expectation*. More often than not, though, God wanted to heal *them*. In other words, they wanted healing on the outside, but God wanted to heal something deeper on the inside (sounds like Naaman, huh?). When I would tell the kids this, they would get frustrated with me and with God, then they would run to another relationship with the same problem.

It was hard to watch these students be limited by their expectations. It was even harder knowing they wanted a quick fix (magic trick) not an inward change (miracle). Though it's fun for me to pick on high school kids, we can *all* have expectations that limit what God does in our life. It's pride in us that says, "God, I know better. You need to work this way."

Could God be working in a way different from how you expected? Could God be seeking to do a miracle where you want a magic trick? If so, please, put the pride aside and know that God is who works in you so that you become something you never could have become in your own strength. Don't get angry at God. Trust Him. He wants what is best for you!

MAGIC OR MIRACLE?

God knew what Naaman needed more than anyone, including Naaman. Naaman's expectation was for God to *"wave His hand"* and make the leprosy go away (2 Kings 5:11). That even sounds like a magic trick! Can't you see it? A magician *waving his hand* and saying, "Vanish!" That was Naaman's plan!

But God's plan was for Naaman to face his pride when the king didn't greet Naaman and Elisha didn't meet Naaman and Naaman was told to go take a dip in the gross, dirty river. Why? Because Naaman had to get rid of pride if he was ever going to *really* improve. There was an inward problem having outward effects. That's true of you and me too.

When comparing a magic trick to a miracle, what's the difference? As I said to start the chapter: *A magic trick just does something for you.*

A miracle requires something from you, does something in you, ***then*** *does something for you. God is in the business of doing miracles, not magic tricks.* So, what did Naaman's miracle require for him to really improve? Humility.

The Miracle of Humility

Naaman was told to dunk seven times in the dirty river water. Dunking in this river was a humbling act of obedience. But why dunk seven times? In the Bible, seven represents the number of completion. He was to dunk again and again and again until the healing was complete.

So what was God's cure for Naaman? Consistent, humble obedience. That was the only way he would be changed, healed—the only thing that would help him improve inside so he could truly improve outside. That's not often our plan.

When we want a quick fix, God wants consistent, humble obedience. God wants our attitude to be: "Yes sir, I know I'm not all that. That's not beneath me. So I will do it again. And again. And again." And you know what happens with this attitude? God begins to change you, to heal you.

What is the consistent, humble obedience God may be asking of you? Maybe you're angry about a hurtful relationship. God wants to heal your heart from that anger. But don't ask for a magic trick, God deals in miracles through consistent, humble obedience. He will ask you to look at Christ on the Cross and admit that forgiveness isn't beneath you. He'll ask you to dunk in the river of forgiveness. Then do it again. And again. Another week. Another month. Another year. Until you get up and say, "Thank You, God. Now that my pride is gone, the anger is gone."

God wants to help people finally find true friendships. I feel so badly for those who feel like they don't have friends who "get them," who understand them. God can help with that! However, please don't ask God to do a magic trick. God provides miracles on the other side of your humility and obedience. He may ask you to put away the facade that you have it all together. He may ask you to stop telling everyone you're fine then get angry because no one understands. He may ask you to show up to the event afraid, even with your social anxiety. It's through our consistent, humble "Yes" that God begins to change us from the inside out.

Putting It Together

Do you see how this spiritual matter deeply affects improving your practical skill set? At the end of the day, here's how the spiritual and practical are connected:

- Pride uses my strengths to hide my needs. That means I can't be *transparent*.
- Pride limits my expectations. That means I can't be *taught*.

Because pride keeps me from being *transparent* and *taught*, it will keep me from being *transformed*.

We're all trying to improve in different areas. Some are trying to improve our skill set to be better at work. Some are trying to improve in our anger management to be a better parent. Some are even trying to eliminate addictive behaviors such as pornography or alcohol abuse, because those behaviors damage relationships. Everyone has different areas they want to improve, but everyone's journey involves the need for intense humility. Everyone's journey involves being *transparent* about weakness, being *taught* by someone further ahead, then being *transformed* by grace. Pride resists all of those aspects of improvement.

I pastored a man who was very angry. He thought he knew best and would let me know very quickly if he disagreed with me. His life had a pattern of going from job to job, having a fall out, and blaming his termination on the boss's ignorance. When he served at church, he was the "mature one" who knew best. It was clear to me that this man had an inward problem that was affecting everything on the outside. He wasn't improving. He was stagnant at best.

Unfortunately, this man had a tough childhood. He had been abused as a kid and had built walls up to appear strong in his older age. He was a strong, talented man, but his areas of weakness were hidden. He didn't want to be transparent about what was going on in his heart. As talented as he was, he was using his strengths to hide his needs. He expected this wound to heal as people validated what a smart, hard worker he was. However, anytime he had to be corrected, he took it as a personal attack. He wasn't transparent, he couldn't be taught, and there was no transformation.

There was a turning point, though. After an ugly divorce, this man went to counseling. Finally, he began to show his weakness. His self-righteousness was snuffed out by the fact that he was now a divorced man. You know what happened? Intense humility and healing. He was able to let down his guard and show his weakness. He was able to throw off the expectation of how God needed to work and accept God's new route to heal him. He stopped serving during this time and was simply part of a small group. When he eventually came back to serve, he was a different person.

He was much less opinionated. He was nicer to those he previously perceived as troublemakers. He held down a job longer and even got *promoted*. He was improving in his skills, his social life, and his leadership abilities! Why? Because his heart got fixed.

My friend, I'm trying to say this: God wants you to improve in every area of your life. He wants you to be skilled at your job. He wants you to be competent and amicable with people. He wants you to be a phenomenal parent, spouse, friend, and worker. Everyone's journey is different. For some, God may want you to embrace more discipline. For others, He may tell you to cut the 4 a.m. ice baths and workaholic tendencies. No one's journey is the same except at one crucial point—we all have pride that limits us and we all need to realize that humility will accelerate us forward.

I like to give specific advice, but because everyone's journey is so unique, I don't always know exactly the best advice for each individual—except, I do advise each and every person to *pray.* Be honest with God and be honest with yourself. Who are the people and what do you consider "beneath you." What seems to make you disproportionately angry or offended? These are often areas where God wants to work in you so that you're no longer limited. Hear me: You will improve not once your boss gets better, not once your position changes, and not when you finally get the time. *You will improve when humility takes root, pride dies, and you ask God to do the deeper work inside you.*

The Foundation and the Finish Line

I struggle to like this chapter, you know why? Because if I improve, I want it to be because I "pulled myself up by my bootstraps." *I* put the extra effort in. *I* outworked everyone else. It's too humbling to know that the key to my improvement was in my transparency and willingness to be taught.

It's easier on our pride if we say we *worked* for something rather than *received* something. And boom—this is why salvation is hard for people. This is why so many people would rather be righteous hard workers who qualified for salvation rather than saved sinners in need of mercy. Our salvation is based on the foundation that we could never earn it! We can only humbly accept it.

This is actually the overarching point of Naaman's story. As Naaman was leaving in anger, about to refuse his healing by neglecting the dirty river waters, his officers interjected. They asked why Naaman would do something hard to earn his healing but wouldn't do something as simple as bathing in the river (2 Kings 5:13). I'll tell you why: Because it's easier on our pride if we can *earn* something. It's harder on our pride if we had to be humble enough to *receive* something.

The greater point of Naaman's story is that you will never be able to earn God's grace. I don't care how hard you work, how much you serve at church, how many checks you've written to nonprofits. All of our strengths have the potential to be armor that covers up our real nature and our need for salvation. The key to receiving grace is being humble enough to know you could never earn it.

Being humble is *hard*. Do you want the power to be humble? It starts with the Cross of Jesus. It always has and always will. The Cross humbles us and reminds us that our best efforts couldn't earn our salvation. It also assures us that Christ didn't love us because of our best efforts. We look at Jesus' sacrifice and remind ourselves, "I didn't start this journey with God because I was good enough. I started it when I was transparent about my weakness and said, 'Lord, teach me.' If that's how it all started, it has to continue that way, too."

The attitude we take toward the Cross is the *foundation* and the *finish line*. The road to improvement, for the rest of our lives, isn't through the pride that puffs up and looks down on others. It's through the humility that brings us down and looks up to God. Only then is our heart in position to improve from the inside out, in every area.

8

IMPROVE IN THE PASTURE

What comes to your mind when you hear the words, "participation award"? For me, I think of that little green ribbon I "won" every year at the science fair. You know, the science fair you're forced into as a snaggle-toothed, awkward child? Math, creative writing, and speech classes were always my thing. Science? Not so much.

I still remember the project that earned me a green ribbon. I presented static electricity by blowing up a balloon, rubbing it on my pants, and then holding it above my hair. Like magic, my hair stood up. Looking back, it's even funnier my mom encouraged me in this project, because it meant she was just as lazy about the project as me.

I not only remember my project. I also remember the first prize project. Kaleigh showed how a rainbow is formed. If I remember correctly, it had something to do with light passing through a "prism." The only reason I remember is because my first-grade self made a killer joke about a "prison."

Regardless, Kaleigh *deserved* that first-place prize. If I was her, I would have put it on display. You know what I did with my green participation ribbon? I threw it in the trash on the way out the door. Why would I want a participation ribbon for an event I was forced to participate in? I put minimal effort into the project, hated doing it, and was excited when it was finished.

On the other hand, I kept many other first-place trophies. My sports teams won several tournaments. You better believe I kept those trophies. When I was 8, I won the speech competition by reciting "The Boy Who Cried Wolf." I even won the math olympics (yes, that's a thing). As nerdy as some of that stuff was, I was proud of those trophies. Why? I put the work in and it paid off.

I say all that to say: *To work hard and do a job well is a God-given desire.* Even as a child I understood how dignifying a job well done could be. I personally believe every human being wants to be great at what they put effort into. Unfortunately for many of us, we feel like the place where we are is more of a "science fair." It's something we *have* to do, but not ultimately where we feel called to end up.

That's why I'm going to spend the rest of the chapter talking about David. Not David the king, but David the *shepherd*. David spent so much of his time in the pasture, but he was called to the throne. He too had "science fair" seasons, if you will. He was forced to watch sheep. Yet, looking closely at David's life, you can see how being great at what he did, even in the pasture, was a key that opened doors to his God-given destiny. I'm warning you, being great at what you do in your pasture is a key that opens doors to your God-given destiny as well.

What's a Shepherd Have to Do with a King?

In 1 Samuel 16, David is anointed to be the king of Israel. Yet, after he's anointed to be the king, he goes right back to the pasture to tend sheep. It would be *years* before he ever sat on the throne. Surely David must have thought, *What am I doing out here? I'm supposed to be the king! What does a shepherd have to do with a king?* Nevertheless, David chose to improve every day watching sheep. Improve in what, exactly?

In David's day, shepherds were often trained in several skill sets. They often played musical instruments to calm their sheep and scare off predators. Further, if they couldn't scare off predators, they were trained in some protective skills, like using a club and a slingshot. Did these skills directly pertain to something a king had to do? No. Not at all. However, by developing these skills *in the pasture*, David prepared for every step he would take toward ruling the kingdom someday.

I will show you how these skills prepared him for the kingdom in a moment, but first: What is your pasture? Where are you now that seems unrelated to where you feel ultimately called to be? *Many people waste the wait because they can't see how the pasture they're in has to do with the promise God gave them.*

Maybe you feel called to be a nurse, but right now you're working at AT&T until you have finances saved for school. Maybe you're called to be in social work, but right now you're bagging groceries. The more I talk to people, the more I see that many view their current position as a stepping stone to something else. David shows us at least two principles for improving in the wait, though. Here is the first:

1. TO IMPROVE IN THE WAIT, SEE YOUR CURRENT POSITION AS A TRAINING GROUND, NOT A STEPPING STONE.

A stepping stone is on a walking path. A training ground is where you improve. *God wants you to improve in each season, not merely walk through it.* As I said, David improved in the pasture knowing he was supposed to take the throne one day. The abilities he cultivated in the pasture prepared him for the throne. Let me show you how.

Do you know *why* David was able to step foot inside the king's palace in the first place? King Saul needed someone to play comforting music when he was depressed and fearful. King Saul says in 1 Samuel:

> "All right," Saul said. "Find me someone who plays ***well***, and bring him here." One of the servants said to Saul, "One of Jesse's sons from Bethlehem is a ***talented*** harp player..." (1 Samuel 16:17-18 NLT).

They selected David to enter into the king's palace, not just because he played the harp, but because he played the harp *well*. He was *talented*. He clearly cultivated that skill in the pasture!

Let's take it a step further. Shortly after playing the harp in the king's palace, David fought Goliath. In this battle he gained credibility as a warrior and military leader, which was another step in the direction toward his destiny as king. Do you know why David was able to fight Goliath with confidence? When King Saul tried to talk David out of fighting, David wouldn't take no for an answer. David persuaded him by explaining how, in the pasture, he would "club lions and bears to death" when they threatened his sheep. David knew the skills he cultivated fighting lions and bears in the pasture would help him fight Goliath on the battlefield (1 Samuel 17:34-36 NLT).

Do you see it? The skills cultivated in the pasture prepared David for his journey toward ruling the kingdom! David *improved* in his wait, and God used his humble obedience. If I knew I was going to be the next king, I'm not sure I would have improved the same way. *Maybe* I would have played the harp well. But defended the sheep from lions and bears at the expense of my own life? Probably not. Yet, David knew he waited in a training ground, not pacing along on stepping stones.

Are you taking where you are too lightly right now? Are you viewing it as a stepping stone? God is calling you to develop your skills and abilities right now, even if where you are seems to have nothing to do with where you're going.

Why was David called to play for Saul? Because he was *good* at the harp. Why did he have confidence to fight Goliath? Because he was *trained* in combat with lions and bears. What are you working to be good at? What are you training to improve so that when a need arises, you come to someone's mind to meet that need?

Get this: *God often gets us through* ***future*** *doors with skills cultivated in* ***past*** *experiences.* Sometimes, those skills don't seem related at all! God used David's *harp and sling* because David was good with it. What might God use for you? Are you working to be good at it?

Spiritual and Skilled

Here's something that won't make you feel too great: God's not going to promote you just because you are faithful to Him. I don't think God loves green participation ribbons. As far as salvation, sure. We could never earn or work for that. That's not what I'm talking about, though. Maybe you want to be spiritual—I want to be practical.

Many Christians think, *Well, God only cares about my spiritual walk.* No, God cares about your spiritual walk and the skills you cultivate. As Christians, we can't divorce our spiritual walk from our practical skill set.

In reality, the Bible tells us, *"Whatever you do, work at it with all of your heart..."* (Colossians 3:23 NIV). It also says that *"the hand of the diligent will rule"* (Proverbs 12:24 NKJV). However, as the old saying goes, "Some people are so heavenly minded that they are no earthly good."

Is there a skill set you are developing with all your heart just as David developed to be a skillful harp player and a skillful warrior? God uses our skills to move us along in His plan for us. What are you putting your hand to that shows you work with all your heart and are diligent? Who cares if it's not directly related to what you want to do as an end goal. I promise God can use it!

Now before you think I'm heartless, please know I am not alone in this thinking. Charles H. Spurgeon, highly influential preacher and theologian, used to review ministry applications from good-hearted people wanting to be in ministry. Yet, sometimes, they hadn't developed some skill sets needed for vocational ministry, like preaching. The following are Spurgeon's words regarding those applications:

> *Certain good men appeal to me who are distinguished by enormous [passion] and zeal, and a conspicuous absence of brains; brethren who would talk forever and ever upon nothing — who would stamp and thump the Bible, and get nothing out of it at all; earnest, awfully earnest, mountains in labor of the most painful kind; but nothing comes out of it at all. Therefore, I have usually declined their applications.*[1]

Being "spiritual" wasn't necessarily the only qualification that mattered to Spurgeon. Being skilled mattered, too. We can't divorce spirituality and skillfulness. Many people in the world cultivate skills and don't think much about their spirituality. But many people in the church often fall to the opposite end of the spectrum. *Believers need to see the skillfulness of their hand as a way to be pleasing to God in their spiritual walk.*

As I write I hear several push backs in my mind, *But where I am is so random! It has nothing to do with where I think I'm called.* Maybe you're flipping burgers. Here's a new mindset to consider: How can you be as effective as possible? How can you rally your coworkers to make that environment a place where people love to work and eat? I bet God will use those skills you have.

Maybe you're working in a corporate job that is stuck in the 1990s. Here's a new mindset to consider: How can you present solutions to problems? How can you develop the character to come alongside a superior, honor their position, and help improve the organization from an attitude of humility. I bet God will use those skills you have.

Never make excuses to stay stagnant. There will be a million excuses you *could* make. But here's one reason to eliminate excuses that keep you from improving: God can use *any* skills developed in *any* season to move you along in His plan for your life. If you really believe that, would it change how you approach your current season?

Many people blame the season they're in for being stagnant; they think the season has nothing to do with their future and treat the season as a stepping stone instead of a training ground. They waste the wait. Where you are may be random to you. However, nothing is ever random to God.

David could have made those same excuses, couldn't he? He could have allowed himself to think that being a shepherd was beneath him and said, "Why am I watching sheep? I'm supposed to be king. Instead I am stuck in this random, stupid job!" But no. He accepted where he was, the season he was in, and David took care to protect his sheep. Did he know it would one day prepare him to protect a country? Maybe. Maybe not. David practiced with his sling and stone. Did he know that practice would keep the nation out of enslavement to the Philistines? Maybe so. Maybe not. We'll never know. All we can know is that he didn't waste his wait. He improved.

David was faithful to God and bore fruit in the areas he put his hands to. David didn't sit there and cry, "What does a shepherd have to do with a king?" He knew that a shepherd has *everything* to do with a king if God is in control. My friend, if you're going to improve in the wait, you have to know God is in control too.

2. To Improve in the Wait, Trust Your Life Is Under God's Sovereignty, Not Random Circumstance.

What could have seemed random to David was intentional to God. Where David could have only seen random circumstance, God displayed sovereign control. I have a challenge for you: Go through David's story and highlight every time God did something sovereignly that helped David along his journey. I'll give you a little glimpse of what you'll find.

First off, God is the One who tells Samuel to go to the house of Jesse (David's dad) to anoint the next king (1 Samuel 16:3). Then, God keeps Samuel from anointing the wrong king (1 Samuel 16:7). Then God confirms David is the right one (1 Samuel 16:12). Keep going? David is sent into the king's court because God sent a tormenting spirit to Saul, causing Saul to ask for a harp player to be brought to him (1 Samuel 16:14). Not only that, but it was God who ultimately gave David the confidence to defeat Goliath, even more so than his natural ability cultivated through hard work (1 Samuel 17:37).

The Behind-the-Scenes Main Character

God is the behind-the-scenes Main Character of this story. And I promise you, whether you realize it or not, He is the behind-the-scenes Main Character of your story too. Sure, David was faithful to work hard and improve, which was so important. However, God was faithful to do what David could have never done in a million years with his best effort! God was moving obstacles and opening doors behind the scenes the whole time. Had it not been for God, Samuel would have anointed the wrong king. Had it not been for God, Saul would have never been tormented and sent for David to play the harp. Had it not been for God, David wouldn't have had the spirit of wisdom and confidence in his life.

This begs the questions: Are we moved along from temporary, waiting seasons because we improved and outgrew them? Or are we moved along because God was faithful to act on our behalf behind the scenes? It's not one or the other—it's both!

When you know that your life is being led and guided by God, it gives you motivation to work hard and embrace your pasture. While *we* do what's possible, we know *God* does the impossible on our behalf. He's the behind-the-scenes Main Character in our life!

I know the pasture is hard. I know it feels like it's going to be *forever* until your name is called to move along. But God hasn't forgotten about you. Let me encourage you with something my mom always tells me: "God's got your number."

God's Got Your Number

About three years ago, phone call after phone call, I expressed frustrations about my season to my mom. No one was doing anything "wrong." I was at a *great* church. I just knew there was something else coming. I knew I was going to plant a church. I didn't know when. I didn't know where. Me, an OCD planner, would complain, "Mom, how do I know *where* to go? How do I know *when* to go?" She would say the same thing, "You don't know. But God's got your number."

Through much prayer I realized, my job wasn't to move along. My job was to WAIT (watch, act, improve, and trust). God's job was to work behind the scenes to prepare my heart, prepare my hands, and prepare the place I was going next. And guess what? God did have my number. There was a point where, in my spirit, I sensed staying put was more disobedient than stepping out. Yet, it was God who made that sensing in my spirit stronger and stronger in His own time. He had my number and knew when to call.

God has your number too. He has no problem getting you from Point A to Point B. He has no problem moving you from pasture to promise. He has no problem preparing you *and* the place He will send you next. His job is to do all the hard work behind the scenes and be the Main Character of your life. Your job is to improve in the wait, embrace the pasture, and trust that the pasture is preparing you for what's next. Are you improving in your pasture?

Pasture to Promise

This book is a testament to God using my pasture to prepare me. Let me briefly explain how this book came to be. I was supposed to preach at Oral Roberts University. Obviously, getting the invitation to speak there was an honor, but I was up to my eyes in church planting work. I accepted the invitation anyway and thought, *I'll figure out what to preach when I get there.*

A few weeks before the speaking engagement, I was preparing my sermon. I wanted to bring something fresh, and I had something from Genesis 18 that I was excited about. Three days before the speaking engagement, I was picking up something from Reasors grocery store in Afton, Oklahoma. Out of nowhere, I sensed God impressing up my heart, "Don't Waste the Wait."

You see, "Don't Waste the Wait" was a message I preached in 2021. You remember 2021, right? That year hardly anyone went to church because we were all confused about Covid. Well, I remember preaching this sermon with all my heart to my youth group. Did a revival break out? Absolutely not. I specifically remember a junior high kid picking his nose and some other ones falling asleep. I was dejected and frustrated.

Because of this memory, I sat in the grocery store parking lot arguing with God. I said, "Lord, that message would make a good message for college kids. But it went over so horribly last time I preached it!" I felt convicted to preach it, though. I finally gave up arguing and said, "God, if You're behind it, let's do it."

Long story short, "Don't Waste the Wait" was exactly the message I needed to preach. I preached it with all my heart four years later, and this time it was well received. So much so that a publisher reached out and asked if I would make it into a book. (Shout-out to Kyle Loffelmacher, you are the best!) I have felt called to write books since I was 20. So this felt like a dream come true!

I tell you this only to say: I'm not just writing this book, I'm living it. Do you know how many times I didn't want to work very hard in youth ministry? How many times I thought, *Eh, who cares. These kids aren't going to listen. I'm going to start my own church. Why work that hard here? I'll just order 20 pizzas and let them play in the gym.*

Yet, I (*very* imperfectly) sought to improve every single week. I worked hard in my pasture, knowing it was a sacrifice to God. At times it seemed useless. At times it seemed a waste of my energy. At times I failed and made mistakes. But I remember getting the invitation to write this book, and I had my own moment when I thought, *Whoa... the sermon that people fell asleep during in 2021 prepared me for the book I get to write in 2025?* Why? Not because I'm good. But because God is! When I preached it in 2021 to sleeping kids, I now imagine God seeing my frustration and just smirking, "Just wait, kid. It wasn't a waste."

Please hear me: God never wastes faithfulness. We are to simply do the best we can; whether we are seen or not, whether it goes like we hoped or not, and whether we see the fruit of our work immediately or slowly. God is the God who does exceedingly and abundantly more than we could ever ask, think, or imagine (Ephesians 3:20). That's His job. Our job is to do the best we can with what we have, stay faithful, and improve with the gifts He placed inside us. He'll do the rest.

So be honest with yourself: Are you treating your current season as a stepping stone or training ground? Do you rest in God's sovereignty or do you find yourself doubting in the pasture? Embrace the pasture, my friend. God's got your number, He's working behind the scenes, and He is way more faithful than you and I could ever be.

9

IMPROVE THROUGH GOD'S SURGICAL PROCEDURE

If you're like me, reading this chapter's title upsets your stomach. I am deathly afraid of the doctor, of surgery, and of needles. Some of my least favorite words are, "The doctor is ready to see you now." And just so you don't think I am making this up for book content, I'll tell you an embarrassingly true story.

I went to Walgreens in 2019 to get my flu shot. I warned the lady about my fear of needles. She laughed and said, "Oh, it's not bad. You'll be fine, honey." The second I felt the needle juice (potion? shot liquid?) going into my veins, I started sweating profusely. It was psychological warfare. It didn't hurt, but it got in my head and freaked me out. At this point, dripping in sweat, the lady realized I wasn't lying. I got up and walked around, trying to shake it off. That's when it happened. BOOM. I passed out in the Powerade aisle of Walgreens. Next thing I know, I'm being fanned by several ladies hunched over me offering me something to drink. Needless to say, I don't love thinking about Jesus as "The Great Physician" (Luke 5:31).

THE GREAT PHYSICIAN AND SOUL SURGERY

My relationship with doctors and medicine is complicated because my wife is in the medical field. I know that doctors are good. I know that we go to a doctor when we want to improve our health. But still, I don't always like their method for improving, so I'm afraid to visit.

Many people feel this way about Jesus, the "Great Physician." They would agree that God is good. Yet they get an uneasy feeling thinking about how He might affect their life. They resist spending time in His presence or with His people. Maybe they're afraid of what He might prescribe or the surgery He might perform.

I've realized Jesus' surgical procedure is similar to that of other doctors in three ways:

- First, it always starts by telling you there's a problem.
- Second, there's often a need to perform surgery.
- Third, there's often a new way of life that needs to be embraced after the surgery if we're going to stay healthy.

But here's what I have to remind myself: The doctor is always working for my good. Whether it is to kill a virus, set a bone correctly, or cut out cancer, the doctor works for the patient's benefit. Jesus, the Great Physician, works for our good too; even when what He's asking of us seems horrifying.

In this chapter, we turn to a passage of scripture that talks about *how* Jesus operates. It's a famous piece of scripture, and it happens to be one of my favorites. I wrote my senior paper on this passage in college. Many people know about this passage, yet many misunderstand it. Let's talk about how Jesus actually *improves* us.

God's Surgery Table and Tools

If you've been in church for some time, you've probably heard Hebrews 4:12-13 (NLT) that talks about how the Word of God is *"alive and powerful,"* and is compared to a sharp, double-edged sword:

> For the word of God is ***alive and powerful***. It is sharper than the sharpest two-edged sword, cutting between soul and spirit, between joint and marrow. It ***exposes our innermost thoughts and desires***. Nothing in all creation is hidden from God. Everything is naked and exposed before his eyes, and he is the one to whom we are accountable.

If you read it closely, that scripture either scares you a bit or makes you think of Darth Maul's double-edged sword in Star Wars. This scripture is actually using super surgical language. Stay with me, because this is actually pretty cool.

Those words *"everything is naked and exposed,"* were words used to describe someone on the surgery table. Some translations say, "everything is stretched out and laid bare." You can picture someone on a surgery table, right?

To make the passage more interesting, the word used for *sword* is misleading. If you're like me, you read "sword" and think of a big, army sword. However, the word for *sword* here describes more of a small dagger.[1] Not just any dagger, though, a double-edged dagger. Here's why that's cool. Back in the day, surgeons used "double-edged swords." Think of a scalpel. One end had one function, the other end had a different function, and the surgeon would hold it in the middle. He would use whatever end needed to be used at the moment.[2]

Why go into all the detail? If we don't know what the scripture meant to them, we can't know what it should mean to us. So what did it mean? It means that God operates on us, His patients. He sees us completely *"naked and exposed,"* He knows our thoughts, our motives, and what we did when no one was looking. He knows why we did bad things. He knows why we did good things. He knows it all. Because of this, He also knows *exactly* what we need to improve and be healthy.

How does God operate on us? Well, He uses His Word, the Bible. Every time we read His Word or listen to His Word preached, God begins to do "surgery" in our heart through the power of His Holy Spirit. God will wield His Word as a double-edged sword. What are the two edges? You can call them many things: truth and love, grace and truth. But I like to call the two edges *comfort and conviction*.

The Edge of Comfort

First, the edge most of us really like is comfort. God is so good to comfort us in our time of need. Maybe you've experienced this. Maybe you've come out of a really hard season. You feel tired. You don't know how you're going to continue. Then you read a passage such as Matthew 11:28-29 (NIV):

> Come to me, all you who are weary and burdened, and I will give you rest. Take my yoke upon you and learn from me, for I am gentle and humble in heart, and you will find rest for your souls.

Ah, chicken soup for the soul. God's Word works to remind you that it's going to be okay.

Maybe you're just beating yourself up for a sin you committed. You know it was stupid. You're mad at yourself, you're sad you hurt those around you, and you're grieved that you didn't trust God. Then all of a sudden you read 1 John 1:9 (NLT):

> But if we confess our sins to him, he is faithful and just to forgive us our sins and to cleanse us from all wickedness.

Again, it's like a warm blanket. All of a sudden you're resting safe and secure. You know that the God of the world, who has all power and authority, is on your team. He loves you. He calls you His own.

There have been countless times when I am feeling overwhelmed and defeated. However, when I pray and worship, a weight is lifted off my shoulders. I throw my hands up in surrender to God, and I sing out words of worship and meditate on His Word. I can't explain it, but the Holy Spirit really gets hold of my heart and assures me of His grace. I love the edge of comfort. I *need* the edge of comfort. Yet, that's only one edge of His sharp two-edged surgical tool.

The Edge of Conviction

The Lord doesn't just *comfort* us, He *convicts* us, too. Maybe you've come home from a long day, you're annoyed with your boss, and you want to gossip about it to your friend. You want to say those things you daydream of saying in that hypothetical scenario where you resign, tell your boss off, and are applauded by your coworkers as you leave. Instead, you feel this little conviction that reminds you of James 1:19 (NIV):

> My dear brothers and sisters, take note of this: Everyone should be quick to listen, slow to speak and slow to become angry.

What happened to the comfort? It's not that the love of God has now vanished. Quite the opposite! It's that the Surgeon knows what's best for your healing and loves you enough to make sure you get it.

Maybe you are hanging with your unchurched friend (I hope you have some of those, by the way). All of a sudden, a biblical topic comes up. There seems to be a genuine curiosity and openness from your friend to hear your opinion. It's your chance to speak up for Christ and let your light shine. And then, you choke. You're scared to profess Christ and win your friend for Him. All of a sudden, you feel a prod that reminds you of Luke 9:26 (NLT):

> If anyone is ashamed of me and my message, the Son of Man will be ashamed of that person when he returns in his glory and in the glory of the Father and the holy angels.

Conviction grips you, and you are invited to the surgery table. Why? Because God is angry? No! Because He wants to help you figure out what is in your heart that caused you to shrink back in that moment. When convicted, we have a choice—we can accept it as part of the procedure, or we can get off the table and live unhealed and unimproved.

We Need and Resist Both Edges

As a pastor, I often see that people are prone to resist one edge over the other. Some people resist the loving comfort of God. Their prayers are such as, "Lord, I don't need anything from You! I just want to serve You!" As nice as this sounds, it's a form of spiritual pride. To think we need nothing from God is to ignore Jesus when He says, *"apart from me you can do nothing"* (John 15:5 NLT). It's our way of working hard enough, being able to point to the devout life we live, and then feeling like we can enter God's presence because we "kept our nose clean." My friend, that's salvation by works. You will be miserable living that way. No sinner has ever been kept from God by explaining how bad they are. But many have been kept from God by explaining how good they are.

Remember how the story of the prodigal son ends? The older brother, standing *outside the party*, reminds his dad of all the good things he did and why he should have his father's love. Meanwhile, he had his father's love without doing one good thing! Please remember this: *Your good works will never be enough to get you into heaven. But if they're what you cling to, they will be enough to keep you from it.* We cling to Jesus—the One who loves us even before we did one thing right. If you can't accept comfort and love, you're probably trying to earn it.

On the other hand, many people resist conviction. To some, God is a loving genie. He exists so they can throw prayers up and He can send blessings down. The thought of God being stern wrecks some people's whole understanding of Him. They know nothing about the Jesus who flipped tables or referred to people as *"vipers"* (Matthew 21:12; Matthew 12:34). They just want to be told they're loved and they're enough. But they're so misled to think nothing needs to change in their life.

Others resist conviction, not because they have trouble picturing God as stern, but because they think he's furious. They view God as an angry father ready to yell at his kid then storm out angrily. This isn't His heart at all! He's gentle and humble at heart (Matthew 11:29).

We desperately need both conviction and comfort if we are going to improve. If we struggle to receive comfort from God, we'll be crushed. His loving comfort is the power that sustains us! Yet, if we struggle to receive His conviction because we think we don't need any improvement, we're out of touch with reality! We are all works in progress, not nearing perfection on this side of heaven. So let me try to say it cleverly: If you only want conviction, you'll be *miserable.* If you only want comfort, you'll be *misled.* If you want comfort *and* conviction, you'll be *mature.*

The Word works to comfort and convict us so we improve. If you want to see the Word working as a double-edged scalpel, there is no clearer place to look than Jesus Christ Himself. Jesus Christ is referred to as *"the **Word** became flesh"* (John 1:14 NIV). Jesus constantly convicted and comforted people to bring about their healing. For example, we see Jesus' "surgical genius" at work so clearly in the life of Peter, soon after Peter commits one of his biggest mistakes.

LEARNING FROM PETER

You probably know the story. In Jesus' greatest hour of need, one of Jesus' closest friends abandoned Him. On His way to the Cross, Jesus watched Peter deny Him, not once, but three times (John 18). Of all people, Peter was supposed to be one of the main leaders in the church! Instead, he commits apostasy—one of the most grave sins!

Let me stop for a second and point out that this wasn't "Peter's testimony before Christ." This was three years into following Jesus. Peter was a preacher, a healing evangelist, an exorcist in the name of Jesus. This sin happened after Peter had Jesus' true identity revealed to him by the Spirit of God (Matthew 16:13-20). Peter was as Christian as one could be when he committed this sin! And now, days after denying Jesus, Peter probably wondered if he had forfeited the call of God on his life. Was there any improving him or his circumstance? Especially after this transgression?

I want to write to two groups of people: 1) those who haven't made the decision to follow Jesus, and 2) those carrying shame for things they did *while following Him*. Like Peter, many believers wonder if there is still hope. We ask, "Can I still have God's Plan A for my life? Can God pick me back up, help me improve, and transform me so that this bad season doesn't have the final say?" I came with good news. The answer to all those questions is a resounding "YES!" You haven't done too much. You haven't gone too far. People may try to disqualify you, but guess what? People never qualified you. *God* called you, *God* qualifies you, and *God* is the One who will help you back up onto your feet.

However, there is a surgical process. Jesus, the Word made flesh, shows up to Peter after his denial. Here, we get a glimpse into how the Word surgically works to improve and restore. Watch the double-edged sword in action.

Addressing the Issue

In John 21, the disciples are fishing but not catching anything. A "mysterious man" yells at them from shore. He tells them to cast the net to the other side of the boat. Wouldn't you know it, after obeying the man, they reel in a miraculous amount of fish. This is the same miracle Jesus used when He called Peter to be one of His disciples three years prior. When Peter mentally puts all the pieces together, he realizes Jesus is the mysterious man on the shore. What does Peter do? Hide in shame? Nope. Peter jumps out of the boat, swims to shore, and meets Jesus. Let the surgery begin.

First, we have conviction. Jesus asks Peter three different times, "Do you love Me?" Just as Peter denied Jesus three times, Jesus brings it up three times. Why? Because Jesus will not let Peter's sin go unaddressed. My friend, God won't let your sin go unaddressed either. His conviction will lay heavy on your heart. As David said in Psalm 32, when he refused to confess his sin, God's *"hand of discipline lay heavy"* on him. Charles H. Spurgeon said, "better the world on one's shoulder, like Atlas, than God's hand on one's heart, like David"[3]

Are you running from conviction? Do you know of things in your life that contradict God's Word but you're unwilling to give them up? When Christians lovingly talk to you about these things, do you ignore them? Roll your eyes? Smile like you're thankful for their concern but in your heart disregard those people as judgmental? You're wasting precious time. You're wasting the wait. You will not improve. There is a difference between the devil on your back and the heavy hand of God on your heart. Jesus addresses the issue, but right after He does, He affirms the calling.

Affirming the Calling

With each time that Jesus asks Peter, "Do you love Me," Peter responds, "Lord, You know I love You." And do you know what Jesus replies each time? He tells Peter to "feed" His lambs and "take care" of His sheep (John 21:15-17). These Greek words (to "feed" and "take care") are the words for *pastoring* in the Bible. In other words, Jesus simultaneously convicts Peter of his sin and yet comforts him regarding his calling! You see, Jesus only addresses our issues to affirm our calling! There wasn't a Plan B for Peter's life—and if you're willing to accept comfort and conviction, there's no Plan B for your life either. What incredible comfort!

My friend, God is the God of new beginnings. God is the God of love. God is the God of second chances. God didn't call you because you were good. He called you because *He* is good. The way into His grace wasn't through your impressive behavior. It was through a humble heart that cried, "God, You know better. Help me do Your will!" The same humility that started you in God's grace is the same humility that will sustain you in His grace every step of the way.

Do you see the surgical procedure here in John 21? Jesus says, "Peter, do you love Me?" (Conviction!) "Then feed My lambs." (Comfort!) We desperately need both edges of this sword if we are going to get up, dust ourselves off, and keep improving along the way. Will you accept conviction by letting Jesus address the issues? Will you accept comfort by letting Him affirm the calling? I guarantee you this—the only way you will accept both is if you know the heart of Jesus. Peter knew Jesus' heart, and that's what enabled Peter to accept the surgery.

The Heart Change of Hope

I wrote earlier that this "miraculous catch of fish" happened twice. The first time when Peter was called to be a disciple, and the second time when he was restored after his denial. Did you know the first time it happened, Peter said, *"Oh, Lord, please leave me—I'm such a sinful man"* (Luke 5:8 NLT). Gripped by conviction, Peter asked Jesus to go away.

However, *three years later* when the miraculous catch of fish happens again, Peter doesn't ask Jesus to go away. Peter jumps out of the boat and swims to shore because he can't get to Jesus fast enough! What changed? Peter walked with Jesus for three years. He saw Jesus' compassion. He saw His grace. He saw the way He loved prostitutes, sinners, addicts, and the self-righteous. He saw Jesus get falsely accused and still turn the other cheek. He heard Jesus teach on how He was gentle and humble at heart. He saw Jesus love people to perfection every day. He saw Jesus willingly suffer death for sinful people.

So what changed? Three years later, Peter knew Jesus' *heart.* And when confronted with his sin, Peter didn't ask Jesus to leave. This time, Peter couldn't get to Jesus fast enough. He knew the only One who could help him was standing on that shore.

You and I can't get to Jesus fast enough, either. We have so many areas of life we need to improve. At the same time, there is no Plan B for our life. The Great Physician waits for you by the shore. He wants you to feel the weight of sin, only to have it healed by the assurance of His love. Get out of the boat, swim to Him, run to Him, and get up on the surgery table. Let Him wield the double-edged sword of comfort and conviction. If you do, no matter what mistakes you've made, you can be redeemed.

There's still time to be the dad he called you to be. There's still time to conquer that addiction. There's still time to throw off the chains of regret. There's still time to ask for forgiveness. There's still time to take the leap that fear kept you from taking.

Let God address the issues of your heart and affirm the calling on your life. If you do, like Peter, you can improve, you can transform, and you can continue on the path God has for you. Don't waste the wait.

The Doctor's ready to see you now.

SECTION FOUR
TRUST

"Waiting tests your trust. Waiting is trusting, if you wait the right way."

10 TRUST IN TRANSITIONAL SEASONS

Black Friday seems to be one of the most ironic holidays that exists. Before you argue and say, "It's not a holiday..." I'm sitting in a coffee shop, just checked my iPhone, and Black Friday is listed as a "USA holiday" on the calendar Apple provides. Don't get me wrong, I enjoy Black Friday and love a good deal. I only dislike when the holiday falls.

Black Friday and the Heart's Natural State

Every bargain shopper knows, Black Friday falls the day right after Thanksgiving. Let's play out the Thanksgiving scene: We block off the whole day, make our favorite food and drink, and enjoy our family and friends. The whole holiday is to commemorate how *thankful* we are.

However, if you're a Black Friday lover, around 7 p.m. your mindset shifts: "Which stores have what deals? How fast will they sell out? Will the cyber Monday sale be just as good? Will I have to leave Thanksgiving a bit early and wait outside Walmart for the night? Should I wear a bulletproof vest in case someone else wants that flat screen a little too much? Do I have a bulletproof vest? 'Hey Siri, what store is selling bulletproof vests for Black Friday?'" It's just so ironic! What happened to *thankfulness?*

I love Black Friday, but I am merely trying to point out the natural state of the human heart. The human heart is prone to be *discontent.* It seems like no matter what we have, it's a matter of time till we want more. Remember the original iPhone? Many of us millennials would have traded our Motorola Razor for the original iPhone in a *heartbeat.* Now if we had an original iPhone, we'd be mortified. What happened? It's the way of the world. The human heart always craves more. Don't get me wrong, I'm glad improvements are made, but we also have to guard our hearts against growing discontent.

Transition Is Complicated

While many things cause our heart to grow discontent, I want to focus on one specifically: *transitional seasons.* Hear me out. There is something about being in between where you *were* and where you *want to be* that puts the heart in a dangerous direction.

I used to think of "transitional seasons" too simplistically. For instance, someone who is leaving one job to take another is in transition. Someone who is moving from one state to another is in transition. Someone who is going from single to married is in transition. Makes sense. Yet, I've realized transition is more complicated than that.

Transition simply means *you aren't where you were, but you also aren't where you want to be.* Taking that definition, it's clear why so many people feel they are in a season of transition. Many people know where they are is a blessing, but it's not their ultimate destination. Whether in our occupation, physical habits, or our spiritual journey, everyone is in transition to some extent. We aren't quite where we want to be *yet.* That's not all bad. Yet, how we view and handle transition is *crucial* to whether or not we waste the wait.

Here's the rest of the chapter spelled out: *Transition can cause* ***discontentment****. Discontentment can cause* ***distorting*** *of the past. Distorting the past can cause* ***derailing*** *of the future.* It's a slippery slope, but it's a slope many have fallen down. Let's unpack it together by looking at the Israelites. They exemplify this perfectly, and unfortunately wasted the wait in transition.

From Deliverance to Discontent

God delivered the Israelites from Egyptian slavery and promised to take them to the Promised Land. They were in transition, right? Not where they used to be (Egypt) but also not where they wanted to be (Promised Land). The journey from Egypt to the Promised Land should have taken around two weeks. They spent *40 years* between where they left and where they were headed.

It's not the timeline I want to focus on though, it's the thoughts they had along the way. If anyone should have been content, it should have been the Israelites! They were delivered from slavery and on their way to the Promised Land. Yet instead of going from deliverance to promise, they went from deliverance to discontentment.

Psalm 106:12–14 (NASB1995) gives us a key into *how* they became discontented:

> Then they believed His words; they sang His praise. They quickly forgot His works; they did not wait for His counsel, but craved intensely in the wilderness, and tempted God in the desert.

The Israelites did two things that contributed to their discontentment: they forgot and they craved. Let's talk about these one at a time.

How easy is it to *forget* what God does for us? I know for me, it's easy to look around at what I don't have, while forgetting all the countless blessings in my face. It's as if we are living with a Black Friday mindset on Thanksgiving Day all the time. That will never work if we want to live a healthy, happy life, though. That's why David warns us not to forget! Remembering what God does for us isn't just to please God, it also helps us. We should remember for our own good! Forgetfulness is the quickest way to discontentment. And as I said earlier, discontentment always leads to distortion.

From Discontent to Distortion

Now let's look at the second part; they forgot *and* they *"craved intensely"* in the wilderness (Psalm 106:14). Craved what? The Bible says they craved the delicious food back in Egypt that *cost them nothing* (Numbers 11:4–5). So get this. In transition, the Israelites grew discontented, craved what used to be, and remembered their enslavement *fondly!* That, my friend, is how discontentment leads to distortion.

Can you see how they are distorting the past? They remember the meat in Egypt as something that "cost nothing." I want to go back in time, find them in the desert and interject: "Excuse me? The food that cost you nothing? You mean the food you could only eat if you stayed enslaved? The food that came from the same hands that whipped you? The food that came from the same hand that killed your firstborn children? That food? That cost you nothing?"

I'd like to say we are much more mature. However, I'm not sure we are. *Anyone* who is in a waiting season can easily fall into this same mindset. When we stand in the middle of where we were and yet aren't quite where we are supposed to be, the enemy loves to do some of his best work. Transitional seasons are *dangerous,* and the enemy loves it. His first step is to make us discontent, because discontentment is just a hop, skip, and a jump from distortion. I could give example after example, but the following are just a few.

In college, I was friends with a girl who was boy crazy. She hated being single. For the last year, she was dating this tall, funny, handsome jerk. He would take advantage of her weaknesses. He would make her feel insecure. He would push her to do things she wasn't comfortable with. She felt trapped. Now to be clear, God loves that guy, too. He probably had his own hurts and my friend wasn't perfect either. The relationship was just bad all around, and my friend knew it.

Finally, God gave her the courage to call it off. For the first month or so, it was great! She was so happy that God delivered her from what she used to feel trapped in. Yet, as time went on, she grew *discontented.* She "needed" a boyfriend. She forgot what God delivered her from. And in no time, the discontentment led to distortion.

She told our friend group she was thinking about getting back together with him. We all thought it was a bad idea, so we asked why she felt like this. Here came the distortion: "He is so funny! He is so sweet! I wasn't as good of a listener as I should have been. He was really pretty good." We sat there thinking, *The relationship you are describing* ***now*** *looks a lot different from the one you were describing when you asked for courage to get out of it.* What was happening? Distortion.

For Israel, the hand that enslaved them was now the hand that fed them well. For my friend, the toxic relationship was now the only relationship that made sense or felt right. Discontentment leads people to distort the past.

What is God trying to take you *from?* Are you still looking back at it? Are you distorting it because the new journey is hard and uncomfortable? I told a story about a relationship, but we do this with jobs, patterns of relating to people, fears, insecurities; you name it, and the enemy can distort it.

Maybe God is delivering you from fear. Maybe you couldn't make a single decision without thinking about everything going terribly wrong. It kept you crippled for seasons at a time. Although you aren't where you want to be, you're making progress. You're in transition. You are more decisive and more confident now.

Until recently, you stepped out and made a couple decisions that turned out badly. So, what's the temptation? You are tempted to fall back on fear and distort the effects it had on your life. Maybe now you call it living with "a healthy caution." You go back to consulting every person in your life, asking them to give their uninformed opinion rather than trust the Holy Spirit dwelling in you. Distort it as "wisdom." In reality, it's a road back to the paralyzing fear that enslaved you. The hand that whipped you is now remembered as the hand that fed you.

Maybe God called you to leave a job that made no sense for the giftings He gave you. You spent years doing something that sucked the life out of you. It was comfortable, sure, but not purposeful. Now you are thriving in a new place. You feel alive. You feel purposeful, but you feel stressed too. It's not easy, by any means. You aren't where you were, but you aren't where you want to be either. You're in transition.

The easiest thing to do is look back and think, *At least the other job was easy. At least I could work half the day and be on YouTube the other half. At least I was comfortable.* So what's the temptation? Go back to something God called you out of, distort the past, and remember the old job as something that gave you more peace and comfort than where you are now. No, God called you out of it for a reason. Don't remember the hand that whipped you as the hand that fed you.

Why do we do this? Why is it so easy to be discontented and then distort what God is calling us to leave? The scariest part is that discontentment leads to distortion, and distortion leads to derailing. The Israelites were derailed from God's plan and waited longer than they needed to. This can happen to us if we don't learn how to handle transitional seasons.

From Distortion to Derailing

That generation of Israelites never made it to the Promised Land. The Promised Land was an incredible place where they could have rested instead of wandering around. Unfortunately, their whole future was derailed, and they waited all that time for nothing.

I don't want this to be your story. How do we avoid the crucial mistake that caused them to slip down the slope of discontentment, distortion, and derailing? It's really quite simple. It all comes down to one word: *trust*. That's why I placed this chapter in this final section. The Israelites didn't trust God. Look what God told the Israelite leaders in Numbers 20:12 (NLT):

> But the Lord said to Moses and Aaron, "Because ***you did not trust me*** enough to demonstrate my holiness to the people of Israel, you will not lead them into the land I am giving them!"

Trust is a simple concept, but it's a hard practice. Let me explain by using one of my grandfather's favorite stories.

A man walked on a tightrope strung between two skyscrapers. Naturally, he gathered a crowd. The crowd looked up, anxious that the man might fall and cheering every time he made it across. Eventually, the man looked down and yelled, "Do you believe I can do it with my eyes closed?" Everyone cheered. The man did it. "Do you think I can do it with a wheelbarrow?" The crowd cheered. The man did it. Finally, he said, "Do you think I can do it with someone in the wheelbarrow?" The crowd cheered louder than ever. They believed he could do it with someone in that wheelbarrow and they wanted to see it be done. That is, until the man looked back down and yelled, "Okay then, who wants to get in?" The crowd went silent. Turns out they didn't really trust he could do it.

Trust is scary. *Trust isn't screaming in excitement about what God can do in your life. Trust is stepping out at* ***your expense*** *because you really believe He can do it.* Everyone can shout. Few actually trust. It's easy to cheer; it's hard to get in the wheelbarrow. The Israelites didn't truly trust. They grew discontented, they distorted the past, and they derailed themselves from what God had for them. In turn, 40 years of waiting was wasted.

What will you do? Cheer cheaply or trust costly? The heart of this whole book is about trusting God. It's about stepping out and actually *doing something.* Whether it's watching, acting, or improving, it is all an act of trust.

God is moving. Are you? God is leading. Are you following? He is the Good Shepherd. Are you trusting like a good sheep?

Let's find out.

11

TRUST IN THE GOOD SHEPHERD

If you really think about it, the fact that the Bible refers to us as "sheep" is kind of funny. Why? Because sheep aren't all that impressive. We see a lot of Christian shirts that say, "You are beautifully and wonderfully made!" I'd like to make one that says, "You're a sheep." Scratch that. It wouldn't sell. Let me give you some fun facts about sheep.

DIRECTIONLESS, DEFENSELESS, AND DEPENDENT

First, sheep are somewhat *directionless*. For whatever reason, navigating terrain and remembering where to go is hard for these little guys. The Internet has some crazy stories and videos about it too. That's a rabbit hole you could spend a lot of time in, so let me just write about one story to prove my point.

In eastern Turkey, hundreds of sheep followed their leader straight off of a cliff. Over 400 sheep fell around 50 feet and died while their shepherds watched in panic. The 400 sheep broke the fall of another 1,100 sheep who continued off the cliff. The loss to local farmers was about $74,000. Isn't that wild? You would think after the first two or three took a tumble the rest would stop. But *1,500* sheep lacked direction to the point they fell off a cliff![1]

Second, sheep are *defenseless*. Typically, there are three things an animal will do when threatened: fight, flight, or fawn. If you threaten a lion, it will *eat* you (fight). If you threaten a deer, it will run (flight). If you threaten a possum, it will play dead (fawn). You know what sheep do if you threaten them? They run in circles over and over hoping that when the prey decides to attack they're on the opposite side of the circle. It's like this weird mixture of Russian Roulette and musical chairs.

Since sheep are directionless and defenseless, they are *dependent*. Sheep need their shepherd. They aren't animals that are just going to *survive*. They are *dependent* animals. Feel offended to be compared to a sheep? I get that.

We Are Sheep?!

I'm not offended to be compared to a sheep. I know I'm *directionless*. My head starts hurting when people use complicated words like "east and west" (just say left or right!). I know I'm *defenseless*. My strategy has never been to win fights; I'm small. My strategy has been to make friends. I'm not talking about literal directionlessness and defenselessness. Neither is the Bible. It's talking about our spiritual state.

Spiritually, we are directionless. We are prone to wander. It's why Hebrews says be careful not to drift (Hebrews 2:1). It's why we can start a Bible reading plan in January and drop it by February. It's why we can say we love our spouse one minute and the next yell at our beloved about something trivial.

Spiritually, we are *defenseless*. Obviously, we have victory because of what Jesus did for us. But apart from Jesus, we don't have a shot! Our own spiritual righteousness is filthy rags to God (Isaiah 64:6)!

You see, spiritually speaking, we are directionless, defenseless, and thus we are *dependent*. That's why Jesus says, *"apart from me you can do nothing"* (John 15:5 NLT). I wonder if you really believe that scripture. David did.

Even though David was an incredible warrior and a wise king, he saw himself as a sheep. David's ability to see himself this way got him through some of the scariest, most trying seasons in his life. And if we can see ourselves as sheep, it will help us trust God through the hardest seasons we walk through too. In this chapter I write about some of those seasons.

The Valley of the Shadow of Death

This chapter falls in the section of "trust" because I realize it's much harder to trust God in the low times than it is in the high times. Or as David would say, it's harder to trust *"in the darkest valley,"* or as some Bible translations say, *"in the valley of the shadow of death."* We're about to dive into part of Psalm 23. It's the part where David teaches us how to trust in dark times. Psalm 23 is one of those "life chapters" for me. You know, those special verses tattooed on your heart and mind (and sometimes on your body).

I don't know where you are, but my prayer is that this chapter lifts your spirit. The message contained in this chapter has walked me through *a lot*. I don't know if you're in a high point or a low point, but I know that at some point you will be in a low point. How do I know? Because Psalm 23:4 (NLT) says, *"Even* ***when*** *I walk through the darkest valley."* It doesn't say "if," it says *"when."*

Low points are part of God's plan for your life. That's not a popular statement, but it is a true statement. In the dark valleys of life, we learn a lot about Jesus the Shepherd. If you go through the valleys the right way, you come out the other side closer to the Shepherd. It takes trust, though. My goal is to help you trust more deeply in the God who has your life in the palm of His hand. Though you may stumble, He is the God who won't let you fall (Psalm 37:24).

Psalm 23:4 (NLT) says, *"Even when I walk through the darkest valley, I will not be afraid, for you are* ***close*** *beside me. Your* ***rod*** *and your* ***staff*** *protect and comfort me." Even* when you walk through the darkest valley, you don't have to fear. Why? Three reasons: God's *close,* He has a *rod,* and He has a *staff.* You have to know these three truths deep in your heart if you're going to trust God. These three truths will help you navigate the hard seasons while you wait. Let's look at each of them.

Removing the Distance

What is your first instinct in hard seasons? I have a bad habit. When life is hard, I go to other people before I go to God. I call my wife, I call my friends, I call my parents, and then I think, *Wait. I haven't even prayed about this yet. I need to talk to God!* It's almost like I've put unnecessary distance between myself and God.

Maybe you're a lot holier than me, but I think going to others before going to God is a human struggle. It's an urge we all have to resist. My guess is that you struggle with this, too. When something goes wrong, you may tell your friends, their friends, and post about it on your story so people you barely know get the inside scoop, too!

Yet, in the dark valleys, David went straight to God. Let me explain something that's easy to miss. When Psalm 23 starts, David isn't in the "dark valley." He is in the "green meadows" hanging by the "still waters." Life is good. And when David is in the good times, he talks *about* God in the third person, using the word "He." Psalm 23:1-3 (NLT) says:

> The Lord is my shepherd; I have all that I need. ***He*** lets me rest in green meadows; he leads me beside peaceful streams.

> ***He*** *renews my strength.* ***He*** *guides me along right paths, bringing honor to his name.*

But David's wording changes in verse 4. When David goes from the green pasture to the dark valley, he doesn't talk *about* God anymore. Instead, he begins to talk *to* God. He no longer uses the third person, but uses second person wording, *you*. Psalm 23:4 (NLT) says, *"Even when I walk through the darkest valley, I will not be afraid, for* ***you*** *are close beside me.* ***Your*** *rod and* ***your*** *staff protect and comfort me."*

Why do I feel the need to give a grammar lesson? Because David shows that in the dark valleys, it is especially important to go straight to God. I'm not saying don't talk to other people, but I am saying go to God first. He is close by. He is going to provide comfort and care that others can't. He alone can give that *"peace that surpasses all understanding"* (Philippians 4:7 NKJV).

Life's Hard Seasons

During life's hard seasons we must:

1. Remove all *distance* between ourselves and God.
2. Remember God's *defense.*
3. Rely on God's *direction.*

Let's look at each of these remedies individually.

1. Remove All Distance.

Try to answer this question honestly: Where do you go in hard seasons? When you go through heartbreak, do you pray first or talk about it with your friends? When you are feeling depressed, do you go to God's Word or do you numb out on social media scroll after scroll after scroll? When you're faced with a big decision, do you pray about it or just worry about it to others? If I'm being honest, going to God isn't always my first inclination.

I'm not saying that it's bad to talk to friends, get on social media, or anything like that. I'm just saying that prayer should always be our first response—not our last resort. We *have to* learn to remove the distance and go straight to God, because here's the thing: In the *darkest valley*, we can't see clearly. *And when we can't see clearly, we have to stay close.*

Dark seasons have a way of effecting our vision, don't they? When you are backstabbed by a friend, it's hard to see clearly, isn't it? Instead of walking in forgiveness like we know we should, it seems better to plot our revenge. When someone breaks your heart, it's hard to see clearly, isn't it? It seems better to gossip about that person and jump into another relationship just to make them angry. In dark valleys, we can make dumb decisions because we can't see clearly! And since we can't see clearly, we have to stay close.

Why stay close to God? Why not do our own thing? After all, if God really cared, would He really let us go through the dark valley in the first place? David stayed close to God in hard times because he knew the shepherd had two tools he desperately needed. David wanted us to know about these tools, too.

2. Remember God's Defense

In Psalm 23:4, David says the Shepherd's *rod* and *staff* brought comfort rather than fear. Those are the two tools God uses for us. Both are extremely important if we're going to trust God through the dark valleys. You want peace when it's scary? Then understand the rod and staff. David was a shepherd, so he knew all about these tools. Let's talk about each.

The shepherd had a rod to defend his sheep. He would beat back predators that tried to come for the sheep's life. When the sheep saw the shepherd with that rod, I can imagine it thinking, *We're going to be okay. Even if something tries to get me, the shepherd's got my back.*

One of the clearest examples of a shepherd using a rod (sometimes called a club) is in the story of David. When David is convincing King Saul to let him fight Goliath, the Bible says in 1 Samuel 17:34-35 (NLT):

> But David persisted. "I have been taking care of my father's sheep and goats," he said. "When a lion or a bear comes to steal a lamb from the flock, I go after it with a ***club*** and rescue the lamb from its mouth. If the animal turns on me, I catch it by the jaw and ***club it*** to death."

You see how the rod was used? That shepherd was going to defend those sheep. And this is saying that God has a rod up in heaven that He uses to defend *you*. Let that sink in.

There are so many times I look back and know that God was defending me with His rod. When I was 16 I flipped a convertible several times. Yet I walked out of that accident just fine. In high school, I was offered weed and cocaine more times than I can count. Yet, a little voice inside me helped guide me to safety. Listen, those aren't coincidental things. God's hand has been on me longer than I even knew. He cared about me before I cared about Him. I don't want to talk about me, though, I want to talk about *you*.

I'm sure you have your own stories about how God defended you. Maybe He kept you from getting bitter and destroying relationships. Maybe He beat back the powers of sickness and healed you. Maybe He put courage in your heart to keep persevering when it seemed hopeless. Whether we give Him credit or not, God is defending us *all the time.* He cares for you more than you might think.

I can hear the interjections in my head right now, though: *Well, Geoffrey, God didn't keep me from some of those things! He let me get hurt. He let me fall into addictive patterns and I'm still fighting them. He let me make poor decisions that I'm scraping up pieces from years later.* I get it. Your story isn't my story, and I respect that. However, your God is my God. So let me try to make sense of some of the hard things you may be walking through.

God doesn't prove His defense by never having you walk through hard seasons or suffer consequences of bad decisions. David (the one who wrote Psalm 23) walked through hard seasons and suffered consequences for bad decisions. The proof of God's defense is that no matter what you walk through or what consequences you face, there is always hope. If your story isn't good yet, God's not done. The hard times aren't proof that He quit defending you.

I've learned that *you can either view your trials as a "fire" or an "oven."* There are times I have "walked through the fire," so to speak. Sometimes I suffered from pain that was my fault. Sometimes I suffered from pain that wasn't my fault. It felt like the fire was going to destroy me.

However, I've learned that with God, the fire is more like an oven. It's not that it isn't hot. It is!

It's so hot that it burns and I question if I'm going to burn up! But when I keep my faith strong, I remind myself God is defending me *even in this.* God is allowing me to walk through this heat but at the same time He is changing me in the process. He is molding me, shaping me, and developing Christlike characteristics in me that I didn't have before. When He eventually pulls me out of the heat, I come out as a new masterpiece. Same person, but a different make-up inside.

My friend, your faith determines if you're walking through a fire or an oven. You can go through it and come out bitter, hopeless, and full of resentment. Or you can place your faith in the God who is by your side. He's defending you with His rod. He's beating things back that want to take you out. Though the weapon is forming, it will not prosper (Isaiah 54:17). Though you are pressed, you aren't crushed. Though you are persecuted, you are not abandoned. Though you are struck down, you are not destroyed (2 Corinthians 4:8-9). We have to learn to say, "Bring on the heat, because God's cooking up something good *even in this!*"

Do you believe that God is the Shepherd of your life and defending you with His rod? The second that truth travels from your head to your heart, everything changes. You can find comfort in the darkest valley, just like David. God is not going to leave you.

"Okay," you might say, "but what if I accidentally leave *Him*. What if I make a wrong decision, take the wrong direction, and remove myself from His defense?" Well, be at peace, because the Shepherd has His staff too. The rod is about defense, but the staff is about direction.

Relying on His Direction

The shepherd's staff was a long stick with a rounded arch at the top. The shepherd would poke the sheep with the straight end of the staff. It was his way of saying, "Nope, don't go that way. Get back on course there, little guy." And guess what? Sometimes, sheep were so stubborn they would wander off and find themselves stuck in a pit or a crevice. The shepherd would then use the rounded end of his staff, hook it around the sheep, and pull them out of the mess they got themselves into.

Our Good Shepherd still directs us like this today. Sometimes, we start to veer from what we know is right. The Shepherd pokes us and says, "That's not the way. Let's get back on track, My friend." It's called conviction. Even more, just like those sheep, we can get ourselves into some sticky situations. We get ourselves stuck because of our own stubbornness, ignorance, or pride. Here's some good news: God still loves to use the rounded end of His staff, hook us, and place us back where we're safe—where we don't deserve to be placed. It's called *grace*.

Even in our sin and imperfection, God is still directing our life. A mentor told me, "If you genuinely want to do God's will, it will be harder to miss than it is to find." The older I get, the more I see that is true. The Good Shepherd is still directing His sheep with His staff. So how do we find strength to trust God in the hard seasons of our wait?

I've been so comforted by the staff of God in this season of my life. Isn't it good news that when we misstep He will still poke us so we can course correct? And if we don't listen the first time and dive headfirst into a mess, isn't it crazy that He loves us so much that He'll hook us and pull us out? When you trust in Jesus, even imperfectly, it's really impossible to mess up your life! Your life is under watch by Someone so much greater, more powerful, and more loving than you imagine.

As a textbook overthinker this revelation has brought me so much peace. As you know from previous chapters, I made the decision to plant a church. It wasn't an easy decision. In fact, it may have been the hardest decision I've ever made. One day, I remember praying about it. Truly, I'm not even sure I could call it prayer. I was mostly worrying and complaining out loud. It went something like this: "Lord, I want to do Your will. But I don't know what it is! I love the people of Victoria, Texas! I don't know how to leave them. What if they hate me for it? What if I step out and then I fail? What if the church doesn't go well and we starve!"

Now, what you're about to read doesn't happen very often, but it happened this particular day. I felt the voice of God so strongly, yet so gently, ask me a question, "Do I still have My staff?" In that moment, I found hope.

God was saying that no matter what step I took, He would direct me. If I misstep, He will hook me and pull me back where I need to be. If I start to veer, He will help me get back on course. So I decided to leave and plant this church, but *I didn't do it because I knew the church would succeed.* I did it because I knew my God would watch over me. If I was jumping headfirst into a pit, He would be gracious to me, as He has always been, to hook me and set my feet on solid ground. I finally had faith, not rooted in the result of success, but in the love of the Good Shepherd. I finally understood how the rod and the staff were David's comfort. Finally, they were my comfort, too.

Your Good Shepherd

My friend, this is the story God wants all His people to tell. It's a story, not of our goodness, but of His goodness. It's a story, not of our wisdom or power, but of His wisdom and power. Let me pass down to you what was passed down to me: If you want to do the will of God, it will be harder to miss than it is to find. He's the big God, and we are little sheep. He's doing the heavy lifting, I promise. He is your Good Shepherd.

Now, don't mishear me—it will be hard! The decision I made has been one of the scariest and hardest ones I've ever made. I'm in an oven right now! But I have the Good Shepherd. So I'm removing the distance and sticking close. I'm remembering that He defends me in ways I could never defend myself. And I'm relying on His direction. He still has His staff. What about you? Can you trust Him? If so, like David, you'll find comfort even in the hard times.

The enemy does everything in his power to make these hard times scare you, though. He points to all your adversity and tries to make you doubt God's presence. The enemy loves when we fearfully question: *"Does God really care?"* Many good disciples have questioned God's care during hard seasons. Fortunately, Jesus knew we needed that question answered if we were to trust Him in those times. So, as we start our last chapter together, let's make sure we answer that question.

12 TRUST IN THE NIGHT SHIFT

"DO YOU EVEN CARE THAT WE'RE GOING TO DROWN?" the disciples cried out to Jesus, as He slept in the boat while it rocked violently in the storm. Our "storms" have a way of making us ask the same question, don't they? Perhaps the strangest part of this story (found in Mark 4), is that Jesus rebuked the disciples for crying out to Him. He *expected* them to have peace while they were waiting for deliverance from that storm. He expects us to have peace, too.

Peace in the Middle

Unfortunately, most of us only have "peace" when things are going well. If I asked you to think of a peaceful scenario, you may picture yourself at the beach with your toes in the sand. Or maybe you'd be in the mountains watching snow fall while sitting around a cozy, blazing fire. However, when Jesus wanted to teach His disciples about peace, He didn't take them to the beach or up in the mountains.

Instead, the location of His lecture was a life-threatening storm at sea. Why? Because the majority of our life isn't spent at the beach or in the mountains. The majority of our life is spent paying bills, stressing about our job, hoping our family tension works out—you know how life goes. Life is *not* a beach. Yet, by teaching peace in the middle of the storm, Jesus is basically saying, "If I'm going to teach peace, let me teach it in the places where you actually live. Let me teach it in your stressful, scary situations." I think this is pretty good news. Why? *Because Jesus' solution for peace isn't merely a week away from it all—but peace in the middle of it all.*

I don't know you, where you come from, or what's going on. However, I know this: Jesus expects you to have peace right *now*. Not when the finances come in. Not when the kid starts serving Jesus. Not when all the relational tension ends. At the end of the day, if God only gave peace that worked when things were going well, what kind of peace would that be? God expects us to know who He is at such a heart level that we have peace right now, in the midst of our greatest issues.

If you're like me, you're thinking, *Yeah, yeah, yeah...peace shmeesh. Can you say something helpful? Because being told to have peace when life is stressful is about as helpful as telling someone to calm down when they're angry.* I get it. And I agree. That's why in this chapter I give you three very practical ways to focus on what will help you have peace right now in this season.

I end the book with this Bible story because, truthfully, it is one I have clung to as much as any other. When I'm waiting, when I feel scared, when I feel like I'm going to fail, when I feel like God has forgotten about my life and is busy blessing everyone else around me, I've clung to the truths in this chapter to calm the storm inside. Let's go into the storm together so we can find peace in the middle of it.

"Peace" Be Still?

One night, about four years ago, I was terribly anxious. I sat up, my mind racing with all the things that could possibly go wrong. I thought about all the ways I wasn't measuring up. My stomach felt like the water in Mark 4, unsettled and choppy. I grabbed my Bible, hoping to find some relief and peace. I opened it, turning to one of my favorite stories. The one where Jesus calms the storm. If you grew up hearing the story like I did, Jesus dramatically looks at the wind and the waves and yells, "PEACE! Be still!"

I was utterly surprised by what I found in scripture that day, though. I got to my favorite part, and the words in my Bible were wrong! Mark 4:39 (NLT) actually reads:

> When Jesus woke up, he rebuked the wind and said to the waves, "***Silence***! Be still!"

I sat there thinking to myself, "*Silence*, be still?" This whole passage is about peace, isn't it? I've always been told Jesus said, *"Peace, be still."* Did my Sunday school teacher lie to me?

I crept out of bed, and looked up the text in Greek. Sure enough, Jesus never says the word, "peace." He says "silence." So at this point, all bets were off. I thought to myself, *If Jesus didn't say, "peace," did He really say "be still"?* And I found the words *"be still"* in Greek literally mean, "To muzzle."[1] You know what a muzzle is, right? It's what you put on a dog when you want them to be quiet.

So get this—in reality, Jesus basically said, "SHH!" Two different ways. My translation is, "Shut up! Hush!" That night, I sat there, meditating on the Word of God. Then, it hit me: *Jesus restored peace, because He knew what to* ***silence.*** My friend, that day changed a lot of how I thought.

Three Ways to Have Peace

To have peace I realized:

1. We have to know what to *silence.*
2. We have to trust God's *power.*
3. We have to believe God *cares.*

1. We have to know what to *silence.*

The reality is, if I was going to have peace that night, I had to silence a lot of thoughts. Odds are, if you're going to have peace, there are some things you have to silence, too. *You can't expect to have peace if you let any and all thoughts run through your mind.* Sometimes, like Jesus, the most holy response you can have to some of your thoughts is to say, "Shut up! Hush! We're not going there today." As believers, we have to get good at this, because the devil loves to whisper little lies in our ears. He disguises them as "half-truths" or "logical thinking," but really they are whispers to take your mind off of God.

I know how the devil works. You're about to have a great day! Then all the sudden, the little voice creeps in: "How could you blow up on your kids like that yesterday? They're never going to take you seriously. You'll be lucky if they talk to you after they turn 18." Then all of a sudden, a wave of anxiety comes over you. Can I tell you the holiest response in that moment? "Shut up! Hush!" Or what about this little lie: "You're getting older. Shouldn't you be further ahead by now? Life has passed you by. You'll die short of the potential you know you had." Then the anxiety starts to set in. Want to guess the holiest response you could have there? You guessed it: "Shut up! Hush! We're not doing that today!"

Rebuke and Replace

There's a formula I use called "rebuke and replace." Basically, when I catch a bad thought, I rebuke it. That means I tell it to, "Shut up! Hush!" There is a second step, though. After I rebuke the thought, I then "replace" it with truth from God's Word. This is why we *must* know the Word of God!

I didn't make this formula up, by the way. We see Jesus use this formula against Satan while Jesus was tempted in the wilderness.

Jesus would rebuke Satan, and then He quoted scripture back to him (Matthew 4:1-11). Three different times Satan tried, three different times Satan failed. Why? Jesus knew how to rebuke and replace. We have this power, too. Yet, if we're going to have peace right now, we have to take those thoughts that are against the Word of God, rebuke them, and replace them with what God says to be true.

Putting It Together

I'm going to tell you a story that makes this truth a vivid reality. However, I need you to not think I'm weird, okay? Cool. When I was 20 years old, I was at a youth summer camp. I was there to play drums, but also the guy in charge asked if I'd preach one of the morning services. If you're unfamiliar with youth camp, me preaching the morning service meant that I wasn't very good but the pastor wanted the morning off. Anyway, I preached my best, and that night I went back to drumming.

When I was drumming, some people came to me and asked if I could pray for a student. I thought it strange that they wanted me to do this, but in between songs, I swapped out with another drummer and set out to find the kid in need of prayer. I was not prepared for what I was about to walk into.

The leaders took me to a back room, where I found a kid who was possessed by a demon. For the record, this is not something I see very often. In fact, at this point in my life, this was the first time I was ever asked to help with something like this. I was *scared.* This kid was speaking in a voice that wasn't his own. He was even talking about people in the room who he didn't know, accusing them of sins they had committed in the past.

I went to pray over this kid, and I asked God to get this stupid demon out of there!

Unfortunately, nothing was happening. I felt like a spiritual infant, and I was super embarrassed that I couldn't help. I didn't know what else to do, so I left the room and called an intercessor at my church.

When the intercessor answered (after about a dozen late night calls), I explained the situation. I said, "I don't know what to do! The kid is demon possessed and I'm praying over him..." The intercessor interrupted me. "What are you praying over him for? The Bible doesn't tell you to pray over it. It tells you to *cast it out!*" (Again, I felt like a spiritual infant).

I had a new direction. I was to go in there and cast this thing out. However, right before I hung up, the intercessor said one of the most profound things I have ever learned when it comes to spiritual warfare. Right before I hung up, he said, "Wait, Geoffrey! I forgot to tell you, whatever you do, don't let that demon *speak.* You see, Satan knows he has been defeated. Christ won our victory and gave us power and right standing with God. So now, the only thing that the enemy can do is get in your head. He will lie. He will divert your attention from God. He will accuse you. He has a million strategies but none of them work if you tell him to be *silent.*"

I hung up and went back with a new strategy. I began to cast the demon out. The demon tried to talk, to which I responded, "Be quiet! You're not allowed to speak anymore." After about three minutes, the demon left, and that child was freed from demonic possession.

I tell you that story to say this: The enemy is not just speaking to those who are demonically possessed. The enemy is speaking to anyone and everyone who will listen! How many thoughts in your mind right now are from God? How many are from the enemy? If you're scared, do you really think God is putting your attention on what might go wrong? You may not be sure how you're going to get from one season to another, but do you really think God wants you to feel hopelessly stuck? You may have committed that sin, but do you think God is accusing you and making you feel like a fraud? No! The enemy is the one who bombards you with negativity and guilt. If you want peace, you need to do what Jesus did. You must look at your storm and say, "Shut up! Hush!" I think there are a lot of thoughts in our mind that have nothing to do with the way God would ask us to think.

Maybe right now you're thinking, *They're thoughts, though! How do I just not think about them?!* I get it. My grandfather used to say, "Thoughts are like birds. You can't keep them from flying over your head. But you can keep them from building a nest in your hair." What thoughts have you allowed to nest in your hair? I'm not saying you will never have a bad thought. I'm simply asking you to watch what you meditate on. What negative and ungodly thoughts have cozied up and overstayed?

If the disciples were going to experience peace in their storm, they needed to know how to silence the storm like Jesus did. Jesus issues a little, "Shut up, hush!" And did you notice the magnitude to which the storm listened? Immediately. The same is true for you too. Take control of your thoughts, rebuke, and replace and enjoy peace.

Trust God's Strength

Jesus rebuked the wind and the waves. Then the Bible says *"Suddenly the wind **stopped**, and there was a **great calm**"* (Mark 4:39 NLT). Did you catch that? It would have been crazy enough if the wind died down. However, the Bible mentions that not only did the wind stop but the waves stopped too! There was a great calm!

That's not how waves work, right? Have you ever been to a wave pool? Even when they shut off the wave pool, do the waves just "stop." No. They keep going until they *eventually* die out. Yet Jesus is so strong that He utters a quick, "Shut up! Hush!" and the wind and the waves straighten up like two boys who get caught playing in class. The Bible is trying to make a point about the power that Jesus had.

If you are going to have peace, you can't *just* know what to silence; it's not just about what you get *out of* your mind. It's also about what you *put into* your mind. This story is begging us to meditate on the power of our God!

2. We have to trust God's *power*.

Without God's power, we're defenseless. Have you ever noticed that when it comes to the elements of nature, we're pretty defenseless? When water, wind, earth, or fire want to completely rage, what can human beings really do? What could the people of Houston do when Hurricane Harvey came? Leave. That's it. What can you really do in an uncontrollable wildfire? Evacuate! That's it. What about an earthquake? Your shotgun may provide peace in a home invasion, but not in an earthquake. The elements of nature make humans feel so defenseless. Yet, Jesus' power is so incredible that with a short sentence He stills what we could never stop.

What would happen if you let that truth fill your mind? When thinking about God's absolute power, does your situation still seem uncontrollable? Because He can bring peace to nature, don't you think He can bring peace to your situation too? Of course He can! Getting that from our head to our heart is the real challenge, though. It was the challenge for the disciples, too.

Isn't it odd the disciples were so afraid? I mean after all, at this point in their lives they had seen Jesus heal the sick, cast out demons, turn water into wine, and more supernatural miracles. Surely they would have known He could do another miracle here. Surely they would have found peace in His power, right? Wrong. Knowing God's power is important, but His power alone is never enough to bring peace to skeptical human minds.

Power brings peace when you know the all-powerful Person cares about you. To a kid, the big middle-school bully is powerful. When the bully comes around they feel scared. To a kid, their mom is powerful, yet when mom comes around they feel peace. Why the difference? Because power only brings peace if you know deep in your heart that the powerful person cares about you.

The disciples didn't doubt Jesus' power. They were calling on Him for help, remember? They had seen Him work miracles and knew that He was special. Yet they didn't have peace. Why? Because the disciples doubted that He cared. One line in this story reveals their hearts' condition. Look at Mark 4:38 (NLT):

> Jesus was sleeping at the back of the boat with his head on a cushion. The disciples woke him up, shouting, "Teacher, don't you ***care*** that we're going to drown?"

Did you catch it? The disciples didn't doubt His power, but they did doubt His *care*. Since they didn't know if Jesus cared about them, they were horrified.

3. BELIEVE THAT GOD *CARES*.

The Storm Effect

Storms have a way of making us doubt God's care, don't they? It was easy to think God cared about you when your job was great. Now the finances are tight, you're waiting for something else to come along, and all the sudden you find yourself thinking, *God, do You even care?* It's easy to think God cared when your kid was 7, happy to go to church, and learning all the cute songs with the hand motions. But when you raised them in church and they ended up addicted to drugs, it's easy to look up and say, "God, do You even care?" In our own timing and in our own way, we have the tendency to ask the same question the disciples asked.

The fact that Jesus rebuked the disciples for crying out to Him used to confuse me. Isn't crying out to Jesus in some ways simply prayer? Yet the more I meditated on the passage I realized that Jesus didn't rebuke the disciples for what they *did,* but what they *doubted.* All people go through storms and we don't necessarily doubt God's power, but deep in our heart we may doubt if He really cares. And if He does care, why would we have to go through turmoil? Further, like the disciples, we may feel like Jesus is sleeping on us too, which is precisely the proof we need to conclude that He doesn't care.

If God cared, He wouldn't let you go through that, right? If He cared, He would have kept your parents together. He would have sent the finances. He would have healed that family member. He would have brought justice to the friend who backstabbed you. But God didn't do any of that. He's sleeping just like He slept during the disciples' storm, right? It's a fair question to ask.

But let me ask a new question: What if the proof of God's care isn't the absence of storms? Don't roll your eyes yet. Just let me unpack the thought. Because to understand the whole passage we have to know: Why *was* Jesus sleeping? I'll tell you.

A Sleeping Signal

I think Jesus was sending a message through His sleep. In the book of Psalms, being able to sleep was a sign that you *knew* God cared about you and kept you safe, no matter what else was happening around you. For instance, Psalm 4:8 (NLT) says, *"In **peace** I will lie down and **sleep**, for you alone, O Lord, will keep me **safe**."* Want another one? Psalm 3:5 (NLT) says, *"I lay down and **slept**, yet I woke up in **safety**, for the Lord was **watching** over me."*

Do you see it now? By sleeping, Jesus was sending a signal. The signal wasn't about what it looked like to *be* God but what it looked like to *be a child of God!* By sleeping in the middle of the storm, Jesus was exposing the main problem in the disciples' heart! They didn't believe God cared about them. Yet Jesus sleeps as if to say, "You guys can freak out if you want. But Me? I know My Father cares about Me. Sure there's a storm, but I know He's going to keep Me safe. I'm going to sleep!"

If you're going to have peace, you have to know what to silence and you have to trust God's power. But at the end of the day, those mean nothing unless you know that *God cares about you!*

My friend, do you believe God cares about your situation? Or do you think He is unconcerned with you? So many people think of their storm, or maybe they think of their sin, and they come to the conclusion that God doesn't care. They believe God is probably angry at them or is ignoring them. Listen, until you know in your heart that God cares about you, you will never have peace.

On the other hand, the second your heart is convinced that God loves you more than you could ever imagine, in the middle of your storms and sins, that's when things begin to change. When you believe He cares, your heart can rest at peace, no matter where you are. You, like Jesus, can sleep through anything.

Making Sense with Scary Movies

If it's all still so vague, maybe this analogy will help: It's kind of like the kid who stays awake afraid after watching a scary movie. The kid lays in bed, horrified that the monster on the TV is now sitting in the closet. Somehow, the kid knows that the second he falls asleep, the monster will attack. So what does he do? He sneaks into his parents' room, tip-toes to the bed and whispers, "Pssst. I'm scared. Can I sleep in here?" The kid crawls into bed, and all of a sudden, he's out like a light, sound asleep safe and sound.

In reality, not much has changed about the kid's situation, right? The kid still believes the monster is there. He still watched the scary movie and still remembers all the scary scenes. Why then all of a sudden can he fall asleep in peace? Because he's in the presence of his parents. *He's in the presence of a parent who is not only powerful but who loves him more than anyone else in the world.* Finally, he's at peace.

This is exactly how we are to find peace in our scary situations. If you wonder if God cares for you or if He guides your life, the following is a scripture I want you to cling to:

> I look up to the mountains—does my help come from there?
> My help comes from the Lord, who made heaven and earth!
> He will not let you ***stumble***; the one who watches over you
> will not ***slumber***. Indeed, he who watches over Israel never
> ***slumbers*** or ***sleeps*** (Psalm 121:1-4 NLT).

My friend, God's will for your life is to sleep in peace. You know why? Because that scripture says God is not sleeping. We're the kids in the presence of the all-powerful, all-loving Parent. As long as our mind stays on that truth, no matter how scary our season is, we can rest. *We can sleep, because God isn't sleeping.* He took the night shift!

The Night Shift

You know the night shift, right? Sometimes called the graveyard shift? People take "night shifts" so that no matter what happens, people will stay safe. Nurses and doctors take night shifts, because if someone gets hurt they want to be available. Police officers and firefighters take night shifts, because if someone is in trouble they want to rush in and help. Security guards take night shifts, because if someone tries to endanger another in the middle of the night, they want to protect them.

God takes the night shift for the same reason. He stays up 24/7, guarding your life. He has His eye on you, caring more about your life than you do. He is aware of every season. There isn't one threat He will miss. There's not one mistake you made that He can't redeem for your good and His glory. He isn't just all-powerful, He is all-loving. And He loves *you*. The second that fact travels from your head to your heart, you will find peace. After all, if someone like *that* loves *you,* what is the worst that can happen?

I'll take it one step further: Jesus not only took the night shift, He also took the graveyard shift. Literally. Jesus went to the grave to prove His love for you. He proved that He would guide you even through life's worst-case scenario (death). There isn't one thing you can go through that He wasn't willing to go through. He loves you *that* much.

He died, taking the punishment we earned through our sin, so we could have the reward He earned because of His perfection. Do you believe that? If you haven't, but for the first time your heart is convinced, can you tell Him in your own words? Just say something like, "Lord, I see it now. I'm a sinner. But You're the Savior. Thank You for loving me. I get it now—You care that much. Make me new and help me follow You the rest of my days."

Listen, I know the wait is hard. I know you may still have a million questions about the season you're in. But please don't ever have the question, "Does God even care?" He does. You can rest, because He's on the night shift. You can live, because He took the graveyard shift. You can be at peace, because He stays awake watching over your life so you can sleep through anything.

Trust Him in the wait, and watch what He can do for you!

EPILOGUE

FORMED, NOT FOUND

Thank you so much for coming on this journey with me. It has been an honor to be a tiny part of your story. Thanks for being part of my story, too. I hope you feel encouraged in your waiting season. I hope you feel more certain about what God is calling you to do, and more confident about what He is doing on your behalf, even as you wait.

I encourage you with one final thought as we part ways—*your calling is more* ***formed*** *than it is* ***found***. Most people hope that their calling is *found* in a dramatic fashion. As if God is going to respond to our prayer with an undeniable earthquake and say in an audible voice, "Be an accountant." It's probably not going to happen like that.

Callings aren't as much found in a moment as they are formed over time. Read the Bible and see: After seasons of waiting (watching, acting, improving, and trusting), God was slowly forming people for what He was calling them to. This is precisely why waiting well is so important.

As mentioned previously, my favorite example in scripture is from the life of David. David was anointed to be the *king*, yet he waited for years watching *sheep*. ***What do you do when you have the job of a shepherd but the calling of a king? You tend sheep like a king.*** That's what David did.

He *watched* for opportunities, even if they weren't the ones he wanted. He *acted* in faith rather than becoming stagnant and being bitter. He *improved*, protecting his sheep with everything he had. And all the while, he showed that he *trusted* God to make good on His word. When you look at David's story, you see that in his wait, God was *forming him* for what God was *calling him to*.

David's story plays out pretty cool. One day it was time for David to move on to his next season as a military general and fight Goliath. When David was asked why in the world he had the confidence to fight Goliath, he gave an unexpected answer. David explained that he was ready for this next season because he had been *tending sheep* with all his heart in the previous season. When the lion came to get David's sheep, he killed it. When the bear came to get his sheep, he defended them (1 Samuel 17:34-36). Turned out that all along, God had been forming David for what He was calling him to.

The story gives me chills. It's almost as if I can hear David saying, "I didn't waste the wait. There were times it seemed pointless. I couldn't tell what a shepherd had to do with a king. But I believed God, and I stayed faithful whether on the farm or on the battlefield. It wasn't easy, but if I hadn't been faithful back there with the lion and bear, I wouldn't know how to deal with Goliath right now. So what did a shepherd have to do with a king? *Everything* because I didn't waste the wait."

What about you? Do you feel you're waiting in the pasture, while waiting on a promise? Can you be faithful where you are, even if it's not where you want to be yet? Can you have faith like that, like David? God is forming you for what He's calling you to. What does where you are have to do with where you're going? *Everything*, if you don't waste the wait. What does your relationship right now have to do with your marriage one day? *Everything,* if you don't waste the wait. What does your current assignment have to do with your anointing? *Everything,* if you don't waste the wait.

God's not looking for people focused on getting to and getting through; instead, He's looking for those who say, "God, use me right now while I'm *in this season.*"

One of the biggest mistakes you can make is to think one day you'll wake up and *find* your calling. Your calling is not found in a moment, it's formed over time. So be faithful, and let God form you during every season. He is working for you, caring for you, loving you.

There are waiting seasons but no wasted seasons. So while you're in the wait: watch, act, improve, and trust. WAIT on the Lord, and I promise you, you'll be happy and thankful that you didn't waste the wait.

TAKE TIME TO REFLECT: WHAT OPPORTUNITIES CAN YOU WATCH FOR RIGHT NOW SO THAT THIS SEASON ISN'T A WASTE?

Take time to reflect: What can you ACT on right now as you wait for what may be next? What do you think is keeping you from acting?

Take time to reflect: What skill can you IMPROVE so you're preparing during the wait?

Take time to reflect: Why has it been difficult to trust in this season? What has God done in the past to help you trust in the present?

NOTES

CHAPTER 1

1. "Greatness," *Wikipedia,* last modified March 21, 2025, https://en.wikipedia.org/wiki/Greatness.
2. *The Incredibles,* directed by Brad Bird (Burbank, CA: Walt Disney Pictures, 2004).

CHAPTER 2

1. *Rocky Balboa,* directed by Sylvester Stallone (Los Angeles: Metro-Goldwyn-Mayer, 2006).
2. Malcolm Gladwell, *David and Goliath: Underdogs, Misfits, and the Art of Battling Giants* (New York: Little, Brown and Company, 2013).

CHAPTER 3

1. Frederick William Danker, *A Greek-English Lexicon of the New Testament and Other Early Christian Literature*, 3rd ed. (Chicago: University of Chicago Press, 2000), s.v. "ὑπομονή."
2. John Horgan, "Discovery of Penicillin," *World History Encyclopedia,* June 20, 2024; https://www.worldhistory.org/article/2490/discovery-of-penicillin/; accessed May 21, 2025.

CHAPTER 4

1. Frederick William Danker, *A Greek-English Lexicon of the New Testament and Other Early Christian Literature,* 3rd ed. (Chicago: University of Chicago Press, 2000), s.v. "ἐκτενῶς."

2. Timothy M. Gallagher, *The Discernment of Spirits: An Ignatian Guide for Everyday Living* (New York: Crossroad Publishing Company, 2005).
3. Gallagher, *The Discernment of Spirits,* (2005).
4. Gallagher, *The Discernment of Spirits,* (2005).
5. Gallagher, *The Discernment of Spirits,* (2005).

CHAPTER 8

1. Charles H. Spurgeon, *Lectures to my Students.* Lecture 2, "The Call to Ministry."

CHAPTER 9

1. Frederick William Danker, *A Greek-English Lexicon of the New Testament and Other Early Christian Literature*, 3rd ed. (Chicago: University of Chicago Press, 2000), s.v. "μάχαιρα."
2. Guido Majno, *The Healing Hand: Man and Wound in the Ancient World, Commonwealth Fund Book* (Cambridge: Harvard University Press, 1975), 356-357.
3. David Guzik, *Commentary on Psalm 32, Blue Letter Bible;* https://www.blueletterbible.org/comm/guzik_david/study-guide/psalm/psalm-32.cfm; accessed May 23, 2025.

CHAPTER 11

1. Associated Press, "450 Turkish Sheep Leap to Their Deaths," FoxNews.com, updated January 13, 2015; https://www.foxnews.com/story/450-turkish-sheep-leap-to-their-deaths; accessed May 23, 2025.

CHAPTER 12

1. Frederick William Danker, *A Greek-English Lexicon of the New Testament and Other Early Christian Literature,* 3rd ed. (Chicago: University of Chicago Press, 2000), s.v. "φιμόω."

ABOUT J. GEOFFREY GRAFF

Pastor Geoffrey Graff is passionate about God, the church, and communicating God's Word so that it comes alive in people's hearts. He's a third-generation pastor who cultivated a deep love for the church at a young age. It thrills him to watch people start to understand that the Word of God truly is living and active. The Word changed his life, so he loves preaching with the expectation that it will change others' lives, too.

In 2013, Geoffrey began speaking at summer camps across the country. In 2017 he graduated with his degree in Biblical Literature, and in 2019 he graduated with his Master of Divinity degree. He then became the youth and young adults' pastor at Faith Family Church in Victoria, Texas, where he and his team saw exponential growth, both numerically and spiritually, and pastoring people became dear to his heart.

Most dear to his heart is his wife, Eden. He says he is highly aware he married out of his league! Eden is a physician associate, Pastor G's biggest ministry supporter, and his best friend. When they're together, life is good. Period. After God, Eden is his priority, his first love, and his safest space. You can catch them outdoors, playing board games, or walking their two rather disobedient dogs. And yes…kids are coming soon! July 2025!

In the Right Hands, This Book Will Change Lives!

Most of the people who need this message will not be looking for this book. To change their lives, you need to **put a copy of this book in their hands.**

Our ministry is constantly seeking methods to find the people who need this anointed message to change their lives. **Will you help us reach these people?**

Extend this ministry by sowing three, five, ten, or *even more* books today and change people's lives for the better! Your generosity will be part of catalyzing the Great Awakening that many have been prophesying and praying for.